THE AMAZING WORLD
OF
PLANTS

THE AMAZING WORLD OF PLANTS

FASCINATING FACTS
STRANGE LEGENDS
CURIOUS MYTHS

Zdenka Podhajská

HAMLYN

First published 1990
Designed and produced by Artia for
The Hamlyn Publishing Group,
a division of The Octopus Publishing Group Limited
Michelin House, 81 Fulham Road, London SW3 6RB
© Artia, Prague 1989
© This edition by
The Hamlyn Publishing Group 1990

ILLUSTRATIONS BY: M. Lesařová-Roubíčková
(colour illustrations, plates and maps),
E. Plicková, F. Severa, Z. Krejčová, V. Matoušová,
J. Knotek, V. Ničová (colour illustrations)
and Z. Marschalová (line drawings)
PHOTOGRAPHS BY: M. Bok, O. Egem, J. Forstová,
M. Holeček, V. Jukl, M. Leiská, V. Obereigner,
V. Plicka, Z. Podhajská, H. Seifertová, J. Šmiták,
I. Tichý, M. Valušková, V. Zelený
Translated by Louise Doležalová
Graphic design by Pavel Rajský

ISBN 0 600 56044 9
Printed in Czechoslovakia by Svoboda, Prague
1/22/05/51—01

Contents

Introduction

In some ways we are as knowledgeable of plants as we are of people. Some of them we know well. We know their names and where they live. Others we often see, but only in passing: we don't know much about them. And there are others whom we see so rarely that we know nothing about them.

This ignorance is a pity, because plants are not just crops, or weeds, part of the landscape, or merely something to make the house a little brighter. Plants have their own history and associations, and their own peculiarities.

This book does not present plants in the normal way, classifying them as fungi, herbs, trees, and so on. Nor does it divide them by countries or continents. Instead, it tells you about plants as part of man's life, as man's friend and servant: how they can inspire and enchant. It shows how they play a large part in mythology and superstition, and reveals their relationship with the world of science. And above all, it shows why man should respect plant life — not just for its interest and beauty, but for its ability to inspire.

I THE ANCIENT MYTHS AND LEGENDS

Long, long ago, people interpreted their surroundings in their own way. They believed the world was alive with beings possessing supernatural abilities, with gods and goddesses, and immortal and unbeatable heroes. People used them to explain what was happening in nature, and to account for the origin of their surroundings. For instance, if they were delighted by a particular flower they reasoned that one of their favourite gods had helped create it. These Greek myths, or stories, about the lives of gods and heroes, are extremely old.

They emerged in various regions of Greece between the second and first century B. C. Later, the Romans took them over, sometimes making small changes in the stories, and almost always adding Latin names.

Legends were later composed by wandering minstrels, the aeolians, who went from region to region, telling their stories to the accompaniment of zithers (a stringed instrument). In this way an immense number of stories came into existence, some of which, thanks to poets, sculptors, artists, musicians and others, have been preserved in our culture, though now they only sound like fairy-tales.

There can be no doubt that ancient culture had a strong influence on the development of all today's European nations. From the narrower point of view of the botanist (someone who studies plant life), such myths help us to

Even relatively simple plant and animal motifs by ancient artists reveal the extent to which they were captivated by nature.

understand the classification of plants, the origin of their names, and their importance for man.

The Gifts of the Divine Olympia

In the shade of deciduous (trees that shed their leaves) or mixed forests, we often come across a peculiar, almost black berry, set amongst four leaves, and sitting about 0.5 m (1.5 ft) above the ground. The plant can also have three, five, or even six leaves. However do not be confused — it

is **Herb paris**. Although the Latin name of the plant is *Paris quadrifolia*, this has nothing to do with the capital of France. Instead, it derives from the Latin expression *paris*, meaning straight, or the same, which refers to the constant number of flower parts and leaves. Although there may be deviations, there is always one flower on a long stalk above four, broadly oval pointed leaves. The flower consists of four outer green sepals (leaves), and four striped inner petals which are yellow. The ovary has four styles and there are eight

The horizontal underground root of Herb paris **with the withered stems of (a) The year before last's (b) Last year's and (c) This year's flowering stem. Thus the plant moves forward a little each year.**

stamens (see illustration, *below right*).

However, there is another explanation for the Latin name *Paris quadrifolia*, which derives from an ancient Greek myth featuring Paris, the son of Priam and Hecuba. According to the epic Greek poem, the *Iliad*, Paris had the thankless task of deciding which of the three goddesses was the most beautiful, and should receive the golden apple of Eris. After considering the merits of Hera (the wife of Zeus), Pallas Athena (the goddess of war) and Aphrodite (the goddess of love), and the rewards each of them had promised him, he chose Aphrodite. Paris reached this decision because Aphrodite had promised him Helen, the most beautiful woman in the world, who was the daughter of the greatest of the gods, Zeus, and his lover Leda. But since Helen was married to Menelaus, the King of Sparta, Paris carried her away from her palace to Troy. Menelaus was so

angry that he set out with his army to recapture his wife. This conflict became the Trojan War, which

The poisonous berry of Herb paris, **which looks like a bilberry.**

ended with the fall of Troy and the death of Paris.

Since Paris had brought about the destruction of a city, the mysterious herb was given his name because it too has caused much distress. Children have mistaken its poisonous berries for bilberries and have been taken ill. The whole plant is impregnated with toxic (poisonous) substances which affect the heart.

The ornamental and sweet-scented **Hyacinth** (*Hyacinthus orientalis*) also owes its name to a Greek myth, involving the son of the King of Sparta, Hyacinthus. He was extremely handsome, and with his friend the god Apollo hunted game in the dense forests, and competed in sports on the broad plains. One day they were testing their skill in throwing a heavy discus. Apollo's discus flew as high as the stars, but it suddenly fell back to earth and struck the impatient Hyacinthus, who was running towards it, a dreadful blow on the head, and killed him. Clear red blood flowed from the wound and soaked into the earth. Unable to help his good friend, the despairing Apollo named the flower that grew from his blood Hyacinth.

The memory of Hyacinthus is kept alive not only in this popular flower, on whose leaves the ancient Greeks thought they could read Hyacinthus' dying sigh 'Alas, Alas!', but also in the Middle East and Asia Minor. Each spring the people of these regions celebrate the Hyacinthia festival in honour of Hyacinthus, who had once been the patron saint of herdsmen.

The myth of Hyacinthus is also recorded in the *Metamorphoses* by the great Roman poet Ovid (43 B.C.—17 A.D.), and has been repeatedly revived by poets, sculptors, artists and composers, especially in the 17th and 18th centuries. The story was even used by the 11-year-old Wolfgang Ama-

The Hyacinth, a popular garden and house plant.

deus Mozart (1756—1791) as the subject of his first opera, *Apollo and Hyacinthus* (1767).

The now extremely popular and widely grown hyacinth was originally found on the west Asian steppes (treeless plains), before being introduced to the oriental gardens of Arabia and Turkey, where it was well liked for its fragrance. The hyacinth was brought to Europe by the French botanist Charles de L'Ecluse (1526—1609), in the mid-16th century. Although he called it the Red lily, gardeners have since developed hyacinths in many different colours, also producing shapes beyond its original bell-like flowers.

While the present number of 160 varieties is not small, this is nothing compared to the 3,000 varieties found in Holland at the height of the flower's popularity at the end of the 18th century. Only a few of them have survived. However, the Dutch are still famous for their hyacinth fields.

The **Sweet violet** (*Viola odorata*) also has its place in Greek legends. Apollo, the god of the sun and light, travelled across the heavens in a golden carriage pulled by swans, chasing the beautiful daughter of Atlas. She could not escape without the help of the highest god, Zeus. He concealed the shy girl by transforming her into a small, sweet-smelling flower, the violet, which grew in the shade of trees. The perfume of this small wild flower has ensured its enormous popularity ever since. The violet has also become the symbol of modesty and maidenly innocence.

The violet was popular in both ancient Greece and in Napoleonic

13

The Sweet violet **is propagated (or increased) both by seeds and rooting shoots.**

France (Napoleon Bonaparte 1769—1821; French emperor). The Athenians welcomed spring with violets, making them into garlands for small children, celebrating the fact that they had safely survived the difficult first three years of life. The Romans also greatly revered the violet, singing its praises and using it to flavour wine. Another likely reason why the Romans used huge quantities of violets was because violet was then a very fashionable colour.

In the ancient French troubadour festival *Jeux floraux*, singers competed for the highest honour — golden violets. The flower was

a symbol of innocence and virginity in France, and consequently was often used to decorate the beds of newlyweds. In addition, the sweet violet was highly thought of by the French imperial couple, Josephine and Napoleon Bonaparte. It was also the secret sign of Napoleon's supporters during his exile on the island of Elba. But when Napoleon gathered his last bunch of violets from the grave of Josephine it brought him no luck, for shortly after he died. Two dried violets were found, along with a lock of his son's hair, in a medallion which he had always kept with him.

The violet was also the favourite flower of other famous people. The poet and playwright William Shakespeare (1564—1616), naturalist and scientist Alexander von Humboldt (1769—1859), statesman and author Thomas More (1478—1535), and the poets Percy Shelley (1792—1822) and Johann Wolfgang Goethe (1749—1832), all loved the violet. And the famous French actress Sarah Bernhardt (1844—1923) was always enveloped in a strong scent of violets.

A sweet-smelling substance, an essential oil containing orris oil, is obtained from fresh flowers. But it takes 1,000 kg (2,205 lbs) of

Violets are so fragrant that they are commonly used in perfume.

for a whole year, then this tiny flower certainly has formidable powers.

A plant with many properties similar to those of the violet, but very different in appearance is the **Iris.** Both plants have a host of admirers dating from ancient times. The *Iris germanica* is a medicinal herb used in cosmetics, and is surrounded by myth and legend. In addition to starch, resin and tannin, its strong, branched root

flowers to give around 31 gr (1 oz) of the oil. And the green-coloured oil only smells sweetly after substantial dilution. Large fields of violets are cultivated in France to provide the popular perfume for the cosmetic trade.

The violet also has a long history as a medicinal herb. It can be used as an expectorant (a medicine used to clear the chest); it also makes a brew, or diuretic (to help people urinate); and it relieves rheumatism. The violet's rootstock was also used to make a laxative and an emetic. If we add to this the advice of the Byzantine physician Priscian (4th century A.D.) that whoever picks the first three violets will be protected from illness for the whole year, or the folk belief that whoever binds the root of a violet around his legs will never be outrun, or that eyes wiped with the violet will not ache

The splendid beauty of the flowers of the so-called 'Orchids of the North' makes the Iris one of the most popular garden plants.

also contains a delicately scented essential oil. The root used to be peeled and dried, and given to small children for chewing to help them cut their teeth. When ground to a powder it is added to soaps and toothpastes, and it can also be used as a powder for skin complaints and as an addition to snuff. It is also used to perfume tea, face powder and tobacco. The oil obtained from the roots is the sweet source of a number of perfumes. *Iris pallida* and *Iris florentina* have similar uses.

The splendid colourfulness of the 'Orchids of the North' is reflected in the iris' divine origin. In the Greek legend written down by the Greek poet Homer (about 700 B.C.), Iris — the goddess of the rainbow — was a swift-footed and golden-winged messenger of Zeus, the highest of the gods, and his wife, the goddess Hera. Since Hera was the daughter of the god of the sea, she represented the rainbow that bridged the sea and the sky. She carried orders to other goddesses, and also escorted the souls of women to the

Iris, goddess of the rainbow, was the messenger of the gods. She is usually pictured carrying a caduceus, or staff, seen here in her left hand.

place of eternal sleep. The way in which she is pictured aptly illustrates her mission — a beautiful girl with angel's wings and a messenger's staff in her hand. Her other hand holds a jug of water to give to the clouds.

The iris' flowers open at the end of May and in June. The six petals are divided into three outer ones which dip downwards, and three inner petals which are lightly curved over three scaly stigmas which conceal the stamens. The outer petals carry a brush of golden hairs where they curve — and this curve resembles the shape of the rainbow.

Which plant has won the honour to carry the name of one of the leading goddesses in Olympia? It is **Artemisia**, a numerous genus with more than 300 varieties scattered all over the globe, particularly in the northern hemisphere. One of the commonest species is **Mugwort** (*Artemisia vulgaris*).

Artemis was a very famous goddess. In ancient times her cult was spread throughout Greece, and when she later came to Rome she was revered under the name of Diana. She was the daughter of the chief God Zeus, and his love Leto, and was a twin sister of Apollo, god of the sun and carrier of the silver bow. Artemis played an important role in many people's lives because she was the goddess and protector of nature, and the goddess of the moon and hunting. People brought her gifts and sacrifices so that she would not be cruel to them, and would make them successful in raising their crops and domestic animals, and when tending the trees and flowers. She was also the patron goddess of marriage and parenthood. Perpetually young and fresh, dressed in simple hunting attire, she was the Greek ideal of feminine beauty.

The scientific name *Artemisia* is possibly linked with the famous

The goddess Artemis, as portrayed in ancient times.

goddess, but it is more likely derived from the Greek word *artemes*, which means healthy and fresh. And, indeed, many of these plants are recognized medicinal and cuisinary herbs. *Artemisia absinthium*, or its substitute *Artemisia vulgaris*, are used to relieve disorders of the stomach and cure gall bladder and remove worms. However, a more effective remedy for the latter are tumeric seeds, the dried seeds of *Artemisia cina*.

Revival of Life in Nature

The flowers of **Spring pheasant's eye** (*Adonis vernalis*) are like little suns lighting up the grassy slopes of warmer regions early in spring.

Adonis had been the symbol of approaching spring even in olden times, and had been reported by the Sumerians, who were the oldest known people in the world. The Hittites knew the myth about the god of vegetation, Telepinu, who leaves the country in the winter after life has come to a standstill, and does not return until the spring. The myth about the alternating autumn dying and spring reawakening is also found amongst the Germans, Slavs, and the North American Indians. However, the ancient Greek myth about Aphrodite and Adonis is better known than others because it was written about by the Roman poet Ovid in his *Metamorphoses.* The myth's origins are not Greek but Semitic. It is similar to the Babylonian story about the goddess of love, Ishtar, and the handsome Tammuz who dies in the autumn and rises from the dead in the spring.

The hero of the Greek myth, Adonis, was the human son of the Cyprian king Cinyras and his daughter Myrrha. He was the most beautiful of all the people and gods. It is, therefore, not surprising that he became the darling of the goddess of love herself, the most beautiful goddess of all, Aphrodite (Venus).

Their love was great and true. They spent all their time together, and went hunting small game in the forest. But eventually he had to leave her for a short while. Then something unexpected occurred. Adonis' dogs drove a large boar out of its hiding place. It flung itself on the young Adonis with all the fury of an injured beast, and wounded him mortally with its huge tusks. Adonis died and went to the underground realm of Hades where the mourning goddess could not reach him. The highest deity Zeus heard the desperate lament of Aphrodite and ordered his brother Hades, ruler of the underworld, to allow Adonis to return to earth for six months every year. So the whole of nature rejoices and awakens at his return, but grows sad again in the autumn when he goes back to Hades.

The goddess ordered a delicate flower bearing his name to bloom on the spot where Adonis bled to death. As the flower was bright red in colour, it was most likely **Summer pheasant's eye** (*Adonis aestivalis*) or **Fiery pheasant's eye** (*Adonis flammea*). In April and May bright yellow blooms of spring pheasant's eye brighten the steppes. However, the entire plant is poisonous, as is the foxglove, and can have a very bad effect on the heart.

There is a delightful ancient Greek myth about the origin of **Narcissus**, whose spring flowers adorned ancient gardens. Narcissus, son of the river god Cephissus and the nymph Liriope, was a handsome but shy young man. He liked best to explore the forests and hunt game alone, avoiding his companions. Consequently, they thought of him as being self-centred and vain. And when Narcissus even rejected the love of the nymph Echo, who wasted away with sorrow until only her voice remained, he was punished by the goddess of love, Aphrodite. She caused him to fall in love with himself and die from vain love. Another version of the story describes how he tried so hard to reach his own reflection in a pool that he eventually drowned. Whichever way it was, when his former companions, the nymphs, went into the forest to seek him, they could not find his body. He had turned into a fragrant flower

Spring pheasant's eye is related to the *Ranunculaceae* **family. Sunlit slopes are bright with its flowers at the beginning of May.**

Narcissus, staring at his reflection in a pool of water, about to be transformed into a fragrant flower.

which, to this day, bears the Latin version of his name.

According to the Greek writer Plutarch (A.D. 46—120), Virgil (70—19 B.C.) gave the name a different origin. 'The flower of the plant deadens the senses, makes a person listless and causes him harm.' For this reason, the Latin name is derived from the Greek word *narkos*, meaning narcotic. The strong scent causes headaches.

In ancient Sparta the narcissus was commonly associated with death, and was therefore made into garlands for the dead. As the flower of death, the narcissus was instrumental in the fate of Persephone, daughter of the highest deity Zeus, and the goddess Demeter. She was happily dancing with other nymphs, singing and strolling in the meadows, when she picked up a narcissus. At that moment the earth opened up and Hades — the ruler of the underworld — carried her away to marry her, and make her his queen. However, the grieving Demeter persuaded Zeus to make Hades allow her daughter to spend two thirds of the year on earth. The return of

Persephone to earth and her meeting with her mother Demeter occurs at spring, which nature celebrates with fresh greenery and the first flowers. But when Persephone returns to the realm of the dead in the autumn, Demeter mourns and in sympathy the whole of nature mourns with her. Leaves fall from the trees and the flowers die.

A Catchphrase of Antiquity

The **Christmas rose** (*Helleborus niger*) is remarkable not only because it blooms at an unusual time — in winter — but because it has other special qualities. These are connected with a Greek and Roman legend.

The daughters of King Proteus abused the goddess Hera, who punished them with leprosy and madness. They ran about the fields and meadows, out of their senses, eating grass. In the end, they were cured by the physician Melampus, who had first noticed the effect of the Christmas rose on goats who ate it. As the Greek historian Herodotus (c. 484—c. 425

B.C.) says, the Christmas rose was named *Melampodion* after this physician. In ancient Greece it was looked upon as one of the best medicines, effectively curing mental derangement and craziness, and also sharpening people's minds. According to a prescription of the Greek physician Hippocrates (c. 460 B.C.), a mentally-ill patient was given the milk of goats that had grazed on the Christmas rose or, in more serious cases, a brew made from the plant. A strong dose was also used to cure obstinacy and melancholy. The best Christmas roses grew in Anticyra on the shores of the Aegean, to the north of Thebes and Athens.

The plant got its name from the nearby River Helleborus. For the Romans, the word *helleborus* was used to describe a crazy person who was metaphorically sent to Anticyra. The saying 'Don't you want to sail to Anticyra?' more or less meant 'Aren't you crazy?'

On the other hand the plant could owe its name to its poisonous nature. The Greek *helein* means to kill, and *bora* means food, giving a combined meaning of poisonous food, or a plant that kills when consumed. The poison is the same as in other related plants from the *Ranunculaceae* family, and is contained in all parts of the plant, most being in the underground rootstock.

The black root has an unpleasant odour. It causes cramps, difficult breathing and can even kill by paralysing the heart. The Roman scholar Pliny the Elder (23—79 A.D.) described how the Gauls dipped their arrow heads and their spears into the juice of the Christmas rose, before aiming them at their prey. However, when they did kill an animal they carefully had to cut out the meat at the arrow's point of entry, in order to avoid poisoning and possibly even killing themselves.

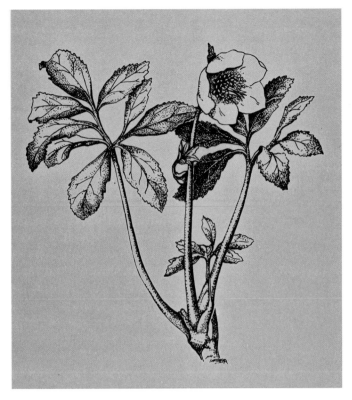

The Christmas rose, **which gives a welcome dash of colour from mid-winter to early spring.**

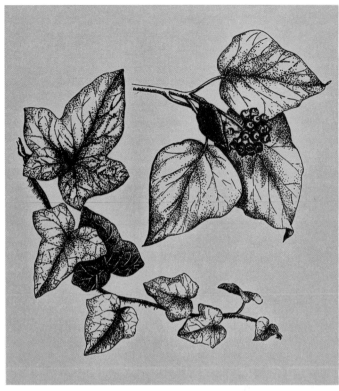

The two kinds of leaves belonging to the Common ivy. One is almost triangular, the other has up to five 'fingers'.

The Symbol of Eternal Life

The **Common ivy** (*Hedera helix*) is a climbing plant, which, with its evergreen leaves, was the symbol of eternal life in ancient Egypt. The Egyptian god Ousir, known in Greek mythology as Osiris, and whose cult mingles with the cult of Dionysus, was decorated with ivy.

In the ancient Greek myth, Dionysus was the son of the highest deity Zeus, and his lover Semele. On the cunning advice of Zeus' jealous wife Hera, disguised as an old nurse, Semele asked Zeus to show himself just once in all his godly splendour. Zeus finally agreed and demonstrated his thunder and lightning. She could not withstand the heat and was burned to death in the blazing palace. However, the heat did not touch her newborn child because he was protected by the cool shade of a thick ivy plant which at once sprang up around the little boy at Zeus' order. To save the child from jealous Hera, Zeus asked the nymphs to care for him. They hid him in a cave overgrown with vines at the foot of Mount Meros. From then on the grapevine was always connected with Dionysus' deity.

Alongside the ivy, the grapevine is an essential complement of the immortal god and his retinue. Later, garlands of the two plants used to hang outside wine taverns, and so became the symbol of loose morals. A more imposing ivy with large pointed leaves, having marked white veins and yellow berries — the **Golden-berried ivy of the poets** (*Hedera poetarum chrysocarpa*) — was used to indicate that someone, a poet or statesman perhaps, had achieved great things. The ivy was therefore held in the highest regard. Ivy was equally sacred in Rome where Dionysus was given the name of Bacchus.

Not only does ivy have evergreen leaves that do not fall, it also lives to a remarkable age of 250 to 400 years. Such a remarkable long life made it into a symbol of eternal life for the first Christians, and to this day it is planted in cemeteries for this very reason. Earlier, corpses used to be laid on ivy as it was believed that devout Christians would live eternal life. And at the time of the mediaeval knights, ivy was the symbol of undying friendship. Also, in ancient times, when people believed in magic and spirits, ivy leaves were supposed to be a protection against magic and snakebite.

Ivy grows naturally in woods and thickets in west and central Europe and in Asia. It is often planted in parks and gardens.

The **Myrtle** (*Myrtus communis*) is another evergreen. It is a bush, which grows up to 3 m (9.8 ft) high. Its historic fame is due to its tough, shining leaves that smell sweetly. The flowers, bark and stems are also aromatic. In Latin *myrtus* means aromatic. The essential oil contains a wide range of substances, some of which are

19

prized for their delightful aroma and their use as a disinfectant. Myrtus is used in toothpaste, mouth washes, in bath salts, and in cosmetics for men. And before pepper was known, the dried berries were used as a spice.

Present day use of myrtle is but a pale reflection of its former glory in its homeland, the Mediterranean, a region of ancient, sophisticated cultures. In olden days myrtle was the symbol of hope for a happy life in paradise. Adam left the Garden of Eden carrying a myrtle branch as a reminder of the lost joys of Paradise.

Myrtle, like the evergreen ivy, meant immortality. Ancient Egyptians placed sprigs of myrtle on tombs, and used the leaves when embalming the dead. The myrtle was also a sacred plant for the Jews, symbolising eternal peace for the dead. And the Greeks revered myrtle no less than the Arabs, Egyptians, Jews and Persians.

One delightful story from Greek mythology reveals the origin of the plant. Myrtle gets its name from the Athenian nymph Myrsina, who was a favoured companion of the goddess of wisdom, Minerva. They competed together in games, running and wrestling. The more agile Myrsina once beat Minerva, so striking a mortal blow to her divine pride. In blind anger, Minerva killed her companion but was immediately sorry for the deed, and begged the gods for something by which to remember the lovely nymph. So, from the body of the nymph grew a charming, small-leaved plant.

Myrtle was a plant sacred to Aphrodite. When the most beautiful of all goddesses was born from sea foam and stepped from the sea onto the island of Cyprus, she hid her nakedness from the sight of the inquisitive faun under a myrtle bush. Aphrodite was also adorned with myrtle when Paris announced which of the three goddesses was the Queen of Beauty. When she won the contest, she named herself Myrtea in honour of her favourite flower.

Festivals honouring Aphrodite were held every year at the beginning of April, under the emblem of myrtle and with heads adorned with myrtle garlands. During Greek weddings, too, the bride and groom wore myrtle garlands on their heads as a mark of peace and love, and to bring a happy married life. This custom of using myrtle to decorate the wedding table and to adorn wedding guests continues in other countries to this day.

Poison from Colchis

The **Meadow saffron** (*Colchicum autumnale*) also originated from a wide area of the Mediterranean, spreading north through the meadows created by man. But while the plant accompanied man's progress, people had no interest at all in it because it was highly poisonous. For instance, the autumn crocus is poisonous for cattle in both its fresh and dried state. However, the poison colchicine does not affect all animal life. Insects pollinate the plants, and sheep and goats graze on it without any ill effect. But the poison can be found in their milk.

On one occasion in Rome a large number of people fell ill after consuming goat's milk. The signs of poisoning were the same as those experienced by a teacher who dissected the autumn crocus flower during a class, but then failed to wash his hands before eating. The poison takes a rapid course. For this reason the Greeks in ancient times called the plant *Ephemeron*, meaning rapidly vanishing, to indicate the loss of life after consuming the meadow saffron corm. Nevertheless, this strongly toxic plant is also an important medicinal herb. With precise dosage it is valuable for modifying attacks of gout. Recently, a substance called demecolcine has been isolated from the autumn crocus. It is less deadly than colchicine and is notable for its powerful effect in tackling blood diseases.

Most alkaloids (organic bases)

Myrtle **wreaths, thought to bring good luck to newlyweds.**

are concentrated in the seeds, which are enclosed in a spongy capsule found in the spring. The crocus then blooms in the autumn. From the corm, lying deep in the ground, grows a long tube ending in a pinky-mauve, funnel-shaped flower. At times the entire flower is more than 0.5 m (1.5 ft) high, and is one of the longest flowers. The ovary lies deep underground so that it will not freeze during the winter.

After pollination by insects, the pollen tube must grow through an unusually long style down to the underground ovary. The fertilized ovules slowly develop into seeds which are carried above the ground, together with the leaf stalk, in the spring.

Mediaeval herbalists aptly described the unusual life cycle of the plant, calling it *Filium ante patrem*, meaning the son before the father. They thought that the plant formed its fruit before the flower. A number of folk names also reflect the peculiar time of blooming, the appearance of the flower, and its origin.

The Latin *colchicum* and the French *colchique* both mean coming from colchis. The mythical Colchis is the Greek name for the western part of Georgia. Dioscorides, who is known to have established medical botany as an applied science, pointed out in the first century B.C. that most meadow saffron is found there. Colchis is also the homeland of the infamous sorceress Medea. Medea, one of the most powerful sorceresses of Greek mythology, was the daughter of the King of Colchis, and her tragic story is part of the legend of the Argonauts who went to Colchis for the golden fleece. Medea is also known to have given back an old man his youth, with a magic brew. In the process, a few drops of the toxic potion dropped to the ground and from them grew the meadow saffron.

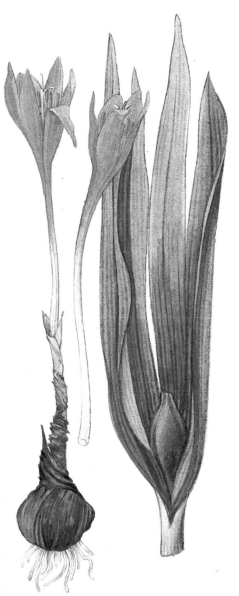

Meadow saffron **blooms in the autumn, though the fruit does not appear on the leafy stem until spring.**

Carthusian Pink

Numerous varieties of the genus Dianthus, the flowers of the gods, grow all over Europe. The Latin name is derived from the Greek word *Dios anthos*. It was used by Pliny and taken over, in the mid-18th century, by the Swedish botanist Carl von Linné (1707—1778) when he named the whole genus. The sweet-scented, eye-centred

flower, spoken of by the famous Greek philosopher Theophrastus (c.372—c.287 B.C.) and the poet Nicander (2nd century B.C.) is most likely the **Sweet William** (*Dianthus barbatus*). In his *Metamorphoses*, Ovid tells the story of a young herdsman who was merrily playing his pipes. His music frightened the deer which Diana, the goddess of the chase, was hunting in vain. She became very angry and plucked out both his eyes. She at once regretted this deed and in his memory allowed flowers to grow with dark centres, like irises. The **Maiden pink** (*Dianthus deltoides*) is a tiny flower of the hedgerows and grassy areas. The reddish, tubelike calyx safeguards the crimson corolla which has irregular white dots. The variety name *deltoides* comes from the triangular shape of the Greek letter delta, and also the shape of the petal.

There is a biblical story about the white dots on the petals. When Christ's mother accompanied her son to Calvary, tears dropped from her eyes. The tears shed over the Crucifixion of her son were transformed into pretty little flowers which are sometimes called 'The tears of the Virgin Mary'. They are flowers of pain and love. Lovers therefore do not pick these flowers in the hope that they will not weep.

The Lasso of the Water Sprite

The quiet waters of ponds and backwaters reflect the blue of the sky, on which the scattered white flowers of **Waterlilies** (*Nymphaea alba*) appear to float. As waves ripple in the light breeze, the large flowers and their circular leaves rock on the surface like little boats sailing out of port. It is very tempting to pluck such a flower, but who dares take a flower from the garden of the water sprite? The water

sprite will be angry. He will catch the leg of the reckless person in his strong lasso and pull him down into his kingdom.

In fact, the plant does not float freely on the surface but is anchored to the muddy bottom with roots and a thick rhizome. The length of the long, flexible leafstalks adjusts to the depth of the water and can be up to 2 m (6 ft). At such a depth and with bottomless mud under foot, a person could easily get caught up in the leafstalks and drown. Children have always been warned not to bathe where the water sprite's flowers grow. They could fall under his power. When plucking waterlilies people had to stuff their ears with wax so as not to hear the alluring voices of the water sprites' womenfolk.

Legends, myths and superstitions have always been woven around the beautiful 'water rose'. The waterlily was sacred in ancient Egypt and in India. Greek myths regard the waterlily as a nymph who, in pining away from unrequited love for Heracles, the greatest hero and strong man of ancient Greece, turned into a flower which the Greeks called *heracleios*. A northern myth says that the waterlily is a water nymph under a spell, who dances every night on the water surface under the light of the moon. The North American Indians have their own version of the origin of the waterlily. A dying chief let fly his last arrow high into the heavens, right between the Evening and the Pole star. The stars fought so vigorously for the wonderful arrow that sparks flew

◄ **There are numerous varieties of the** *Dianthus* **family (the flower of the gods) throughout Europe. Pictured here are the beautiful (1)** Maiden pink **(2)** Carthusianorum **(3)** Sweet William **(4)** Sandwort **(5)** *Dianthus plumarius* **(6)** Chinese carnation **(7)** Carnation.

I. ꝃeïꝛo anebo Sꞇꞈuliꝛ.   I. Nymphæa alba.   I. Weiſs Seeblümen.

A 400-year-old illustration of the Waterlily **(Matthioli, 1562).**

and those that fell onto the water became the sacred waterlily.

The waterlily was attractive to man not only for its beauty but also for its mysterious behaviour. The flowers only open on sunny days. They seem to follow the sun's progress on its journey across the heavens and, around four o'clock in the afternoon, close once more. Within two hours, they disappear below the surface. The flower resurfaces at seven the next morning. Linné classifies such plants with a marked daily rhythm as 'flower clocks'. He arranged a number of these plants in a flowerbed in such a way that they opened, one after another, at certain times.

Granddad Philemon and Granny Baucis

'Once upon a time there was a house in which two old people, Granddad Philemon and Granny Baucis, lived contentedly.' This could be the start of a fairy story, but is in fact the beginning of an ancient Greek tale about the origin of the cornelian cherry, as told by the poet Publius Ovidius Naso (43 B.C.—17 A.D.). The time is known

The Watersprite Guards his Flowers (painting by J. Zrzavý).

used to make jam, syrup, wine, and a Turkish drink, sherbet, all equally pleasant and refreshing.

The cornelian cherry is not only a fruit-bearing plant, it is also a medicinal plant. It cures digestive troubles and coughs, and reduces fever and bleeding. In the Middle Ages it was included among the medicinal herbs of St. Hildëgard, and the Benedictine monks grew the cherry in their monastery gardens.

The golden-yellow flowers bloom in dense umbels (flower clusters) from the end of February to the beginning of April, being visible from afar in the drab landscape before the advent of spring. They attract the bees for their first feast of spring.

The *Cornus* is valuable to man both for its fruit and its wood. The smooth but dense, tough, hard wood is sought by wood carvers, turners and wheelwrights. It has been used to make resistant machine parts, as well as precise mathematical instruments. The very best walking sticks are made from the branches of this tree.

The delightful blossom and fruit of the Cornelian cherry.

as the 'Golden Age' of mankind, when people lived happily in lasting peace. It was the period when Cronus ruled over the world.

Two tired and hungry pilgrims came to the isolated little cottage on the edge of the forest. They begged to be allowed to rest a while. The good-hearted couple served their guests a meal of cornelian cherries, without having the least inkling that the visitors were Zeus and his son Hermes. When the guests took their leave, they rewarded their hosts by granting them a wish. The old couple had

only one wish, that they should die together. The divine father and his son fulfilled this wish and turned the couple into a tree with a double trunk — the **Cornelian cherry** (*Cornus mas*). It is therefore possible that the family name of *Cornus*, a tree with wood of many uses, derived from the god Cronus, father of Zeus.

The most frequently used part of the cornelian cherry is its fruit. From ancient times both the ripe and the unripe stone fruit have been prepared in the same way as olives. The fruit has also been

Drops from the Milky Way

The elegant beauty of the **Lily** (*Lilium*) has accompanied man for so long that we no longer know where it occurs wild in nature or where is the site of its origin; perhaps in the east Mediterranean, or from southern Yugoslavia down to Lebanon. In folklore, however, its origin is thought to be supernatural.

According to an ancient myth, Heracles, the illegitimate son of Zeus, was fated to suffer a cruel blow at the hands of Hera (called Juno by the Romans). Since the famous hero of Greek legend was humanly vulnerable at birth, his mother, the Tyrrhenian Queen Alcmene, hid him. But his hiding place was betrayed, whereupon Zeus sent the swift-footed Hermes to save the child. He put the child to the breast of the sleeping Hera so that her milk would give him immortality. However, the infant bit the goddess' breast so that she was startled, woke up, and pulled the child away so violently that her milk gushed forth. Thus the milky way took shape over the heavens, while the few drops that fell to the ground turned into white lilies — Juno's roses, as the Romans called them.

Evidence that the lily was one of the first ornamental flowers in the history of mankind is contained in reports from the oldest cultures — Sumerian, Babylonian, Assyrian, Phoenician, Egyptian, Greek, and Roman. In Christianity, in particular, the **Madonna lily** (*Lilium candidum*) assumed a crucial position as the symbol of innocence. From June to July, large cathedrals and rural churches are drenched with the heavy fragrance of these lilies, which were always grown in monastery gardens. They were also frequently planted in country gardens, holding their traditional place alongside roses, phlox and

The bell-like flowers of the Madonna lily are famous for their strong perfume.

dahlias. According to another old legend the lily came into being together with the rose.

The German writer and philosopher of the 18th century, Johann Gottfried Herder (1744—1803), a friend of the poet Goethe, wrote in the style of the old legends about how flowers came into being: 'When the earth was still wasteland a group of charming nymphs came to a bare rock to brighten the barren soil with flow-

ers. They at once shared out their tasks. Under the snow, in the cool grass, Humility started forming the modest violet and after her, Hope filled the calyxes of the hyacinth with a delightful and refreshing fragrance. When both of them had completed their tasks, a whole range of other bright flowers were created. The tulip proudly raised its head, and the narcissus gazed dreamily around. Seeing this, Venus said to her Graces: ''What are you waiting for, sisters of charm, hurry up and create the flowers of your tenderness!'' So the Graces came down to earth and Aglaia (or innocence), formed the lily, and Thalia and Euphrosyne together formed the sister flower of joy and love, the delightful rose. Since then, the rose and the lily have bloomed together in one field and mutually adorn each other, for they were formed together by the sisters of grace.'

It is likely, though, that the madonna lily was a symbol of innocence long before the onset of Christianity. One of the oldest preserved memorials picturing a lily is the seal cylinder of the Sumerian ruler Gudea of Lagash (c.2130 B.C.). According to the ancient Hebrew legend, the first lily grew in the Garden of Temptation and it alone remained pure and innocent. In Christianity, the Virgin Mary, St. Aloysius and John the Baptist, hold a madonna lily in their hand as a symbol of innocence.

The Latin name *lilium* is a distortion of the Greek *leirion*, derived from the word *leiros*, meaning pale or delicate. *Leirion* was turned into *lirium*, and from that word originated *lilium*.

The lily also found its way into Scandinavian legends. Thor, the god of thunder, was represented with lightning in one hand and a sceptre ending in a lily in the other. In ancient French literature, the lily was the magic wand of Oberon, the mythical king of the fairies and elves. Each lily is said to have its elf who is born with it, lives in it, and dies with it.

The loveliest of all legends is the fairytale story of the Jewish King Solomon. Queen Sibyl of Sheba, who wanted to test his famous wisdom, once presented him with a bunch of lilies. In the bunch of living flowers there was one made of silver, looking exactly like the others. She wanted him to recognize it without touching the blooms. The king placed the flowers in a vase near an open window and observed them. He recognized the artificial flower very quickly — no bees settled on it.

Hyacinth

II THE MYSTERIOUS POWER OF MAGIC

Henbane

Plants for making spells have always been shrouded in the mystery of magic. Faith in the magic power of some plants has always grown out of certain known facts, such as the shape of the root. From there it is only a short step to believing in the magical powers of plants to work charms.

The Thorn-apple (*Datura stramonium*) together with **Deadly nightshade** (*Bella donna*) and **Henbane**, belong to the egg plant family (*Solanaceae*), which contain remarkable chemicals. According to the way they are used, they are either deadly poisonous, magically narcotic (inducing sleepiness), or medicinal. They were essential ingredients of magical narcotic love potions which were intended to arouse the interest of a chosen partner. Another plant famous for its magical properties was mandragora. In western France a tried and sacred means for awakening love was **Verbena** (*Verbena*), which is mentioned in the old Celtic-Brittany romantic poem about Tristan and Isolde. The all-powerful 'Flower of Love' — *Amoris anthos* — in the 16th century was **Amaranth** (*Amaranthus*).

Nature's magic, concealed in plants, chased away spirits, devils and witches. The **Common tansy** (*Tanacetum vulgare*) could even chase away vampires and werewolves. But much of the magical power attributed to plants was greatly exaggerated and was only sustained by superstition. One superstition claimed that girls growing hydrangeas on their windowsills would never marry. And the antique 'cross-wort' arrow root, prepared from the root of **Butter bur** (*Petasites*), was said to make people invulnerable!

The exotic seeds of the Seychelles palm, called the sea cocoanut, had magical rejuvenating power. In the Middle Ages their stone-hard shells were used as cups which gave drink poured into it magical strength.

However, large numbers of plants really are an invaluable aid to man — as a source of vitamins and natural medicine. The plants themselves are magical aids, maintaining life on earth.

The Witches' Kitchen

The entire **Henbane** (*Hyoscyamus niger*) is highly poisonous. It contains chemicals which strongly irritate the nerve centre, expand the eye pupils, and induce delirium, hallucinations and visions. In the end they cause death.

In bygone ages, the Hindus, Assyrians, Babylonians, Egyptians, Greeks, and Romans used henbane as a medicinal herb to treat a variety of illnesses. The Egyptians called henbane *safti* or *spti*, and used smoke from the burning seeds to treat toothache. The Arabs called henbane *bendi* or *sicran*, using it to alleviate pain and to dullen the senses during operations.

In the superstitious Middle Ages, the curative properties of henbane were suppressed by its 'magic' properties. Henbane became one of the chief components of the legendary magic healing ointments and love potions *pocula amatoris*. Witches, who it was thought existed in large numbers, spread the paste on their temples, under their armpits, and over the private parts of their bodies. The toxic paste made them fall into trances, in which they hallucinated. They thought they saw unbelievable events; they imagined themselves flying through the air; and they saw devils and made love to Satan. Upon awakening, they firmly believed that these events had actually happened. On describing their experiences, the witches won awesome respect, but most of them ended up in the torture chambers of the inquisition, or were burned to death.

Sometimes an extraction from henbane was added to *aqua tofana*, the infamous Italian poison. According to Shakespeare's play, the father of the Danish Prince Hamlet was murdered with the juice of henbane, poured into his ear by his brother. On St. John's Day, henbane was burned in cattle sheds to protect the cattle against the evil eye (a dreadful look capable of inflicting harm). Henbane could also summon rain, provided it had been picked by a naked maiden with the little finger of her right hand, and been carried to the river under her right big toe!

When the age of witchcraft and devils came to an end in the 17th century henbane was more or less forgotten and was scorned as a dangerous toxic plant. Then, in 1821, a Frenchman Brendes discovered another chemical substance in henbane (alkaloid hyosciamine). The plant is now a valuable raw material in the production of tranquilizing and sleep-inducing drugs, and in the treatment of nervous diseases and stomach ulcers.

The **Thorn-apple** or **Jimson-weed** (*Datura stramonium*) is an annual plant, growing up to 1 mm (3 ft) high. The flowers are lovely white bells, up to 8 cm (3 in) long, which have a faint but pleasant fragrance, especially when they open in the evening. They attract hawkmoths for pollination.

The thorn-apple was brought from America to Europe by Francesco Hernandes, the personal physician of the Spanish King Philip II, in the middle of the 16th century. Hernandes explained that he had found the thorn-apple in Mexico and wrote about it under the old Aztec name of *tlapatl*.

The thorn-apple was also used in witches' quack medicines and unguents (healing ointments). The witches carried them through the air to Brocken peak in the Harz Mountains in Germany for Walpurgis Night. The supernatural power of the magic unguents, according to the 17th century recipe, is explained by modern science. The drug sends a person to sleep for 24 hours. But it is a disturbed sleep, and the irregular beat of the drugged heart makes people feel that they are moving through space, as on a broomstick, or are dancing wildly. Although these sensations occur while the person is asleep, on waking they are convinced that these events actually happened.

The Mexican Indians used some kind of thorn-apple as a narcosis during painful operations. It still grows near the temples of the Incas, where the priests used to carry out operations.

Bearded darnel (*Lolium temulentum*) is an annual grass growing as a troublesome weed among cereals, especially barley and oats. It has spread through the world with cereals, and used to be the cause of frequent poisoning from contaminated flour. From the fields it spreads to rubbish heaps, onto field paths and to waste land, where there is poor vegetation. Bearded darnel is a bushy grass which has a thick stem and large joints.

This insignificant grass has an interesting history and properties. Bearded darnel was one of the ingredients of magical unguents. The ripe ears contain a chemical which is formed as the ears mature. It is not formed by the plant itself but by a fungus which is found in the cells of the grain. The fungus gets into the plant when the grain is germinating. It moves to the flower head of the young plant and, after fertilization, spreads to the cells of the grain where it creates the chemical.

The bearded darnel has been found among grains of emmer wheat in the tombs of Egyptian kings more than 4,500 years old. It is remarkable that these grains also contained a fungus. Grains of bearded darnel have been preserved in central European log constructions of the Swiss lake dwellers from the Neolithic and Bronze ages.

Even in Roman times bearded darnel was a weed of the wheat fields and a danger to health. The Roman name for the plant was *lolium*. The Latin expression *temulentus*, meaning drunken or drugged, indicates the toxic effect of the grass.

Deadly nightshade (*Atropa bella donna*) is a perennial (long living) tall plant found in deciduous woods and hedgerows. However, it contains highly poisonous substances, all of which effect the nervous system, evoking feelings of drunkenness, irritability, hallucinations and drugged sleep. Poisoning ends in death by paralysis of the respiratory (breathing) system. The toxins are so strong that even a mere 0.1 gr can be fatal.

The Greek philosopher, Theophrastus, wrote about deadly nightshade calling it *mandragoras*. The word *dolo* in the works of the Abbess St. Hildëgard might also have meant deadly nightshade. It was an essential ingredient in the soothing ointments or salves of witches in the Middle Ages. T. B. Paracelsus (1493—1541), a scholar of the early 16th century, described how these salves contained the fat of children or bat's blood, and extracts from henbane, deadly nightshade, hemlock and mandragora. The most effective and magical part of deadly nightshade was the root. However, obtaining it involved great danger. Whoever wanted to get the thick root had to dig it up at midnight, while a circle had to be drawn around the person using consecrated chalk so that the devil guarding the plant could not reach him. And to divert the devil's attention on departure, he had to fling down a black hen in a sack tied up with 99 knots. The devil would assume

In the Middle Ages narcotic (or sleep-inducing) plants were used more for their medicinal attributes. Seen here are (1) Henbane — open fruit and seed (2) Thorn-apple — capsule and seed (3) Bearded darnel. All these plants were the main ingredients of magical ointments and potions.

the hen was the soul of the culprit but before he could untie all the knots, the fellow made his escape.

At other times the root of the deadly nightshade was pulled out of the ground on Christmas Eve, with similar safety precautions being taken. The root was also worn against bare skin, to bring luck in card playing. The root could even promote love — if a girl was carrying it she could charm whoever she wished. However, she first had to pull up the root in the company of her mother one Sunday in Shrovetide, or on St. George's Day, then place some bread, salt and liqueur on the spot where the root was removed and, finally, carry the root home on her head. If asked she could not say what she was carrying, and she also had to refrain from arguing with her mother.

Sometimes deadly nightshade was used against the bite of a mad dog. It was also given in powder form to horses to make them lively and give them a shining coat. In the countries of southern Europe, young girls dropped the juice of the berries of deadly nightshade into their eyes to make them large and shining. Hence the plant's Italian name, *bella donna*, meaning lovely lady. Also, Slav girls painted their cheeks with the juice of the berry.

Deadly nightshade received its family name from Atropos, one of the three Fates who decided the hour of death of every person.

Ceremony of the Ancient Celts

When the leaves fall from the trees before winter, 'nests' can be observed high up in the crowns of oak trees. They are little bushes of the **Mistletoe** (*Viscum album*), whose ripe white berries are spread, via birds' droppings, over wide areas. (The main carrier, the

The ancient druids used a golden sickle to cut down Mistletoe, **which they used as a pain-reliever.**

mistle thrush, was named by Linné *Turdus viscivorus*.) Consequently there is always enough mistletoe for decoration at Christmas time, and also for making drugs. At the time of the ancient Celts, the magical juice of the mistletoe was used to relieve pain and to ease death. That is why the plant, a parasite in the crowns of oak trees, was held sacred.

According to the ancient story, the wizard Merlin, accompanied by his black dog, went out to find mistletoe early in the morning. Under the tree where he found it, a ceremony was held six days

after the full moon. Then the high priest, or an initiated priest dressed in white, climbed the tree and used a gold sickle to cut off the bunches of mistletoe, which were allowed to drop onto a white cloth. In this way the magic power of the evergreen plant, which grew high up in the realm of the birds, was preserved.

Those plants which grow from seeds at such a height, and without roots, were considered magical. But mistletoe is only partially a parasite on its host. The haustoria (food-absorbing mechanism) take from the host only water

30

A gilded sprig of Mistletoe, which is a good luck symbol at Christmas time.

and the mineral salts dissolved in it. Sugars, and other organic substances needed for its survival, are manufactured in its green leaves.

Mistletoe is also recognized as a medicinal herb, and to this day is used to help older people with ailing hearts and high blood pressure.

The white berries of mistletoe have a very viscous (sticky) content, which can be obtained by boiling them. This soft green substance was once used by bird catchers who spread it on lime rods. When their prey landed on them, the 'glue' caught the bird's feet and prevented them from flying away.

The Scandinavians believed that mistletoe had the power of a magic wand, and old Slavs used branches of mistletoe for various kinds of magic and charms. According to an old Serbian superstition treasure has been concealed under a tree where mistletoe grows. And in England and France a quantity of mistletoe on the table was thought to be a promise of a rich grain harvest.

Magical Superstitions

A very thorny, coniferous shrub, **Juniper** (*Juniperus communis*), has always been a very popular folk medicine, which is used for a variety of ailments. And the berry-like fruits are an excellent spice used in sauces and in preparing game (wild animals and birds).

In the Middle Ages, when there were terrible outbreaks of epidemic diseases, juniper was also

The slim Juniper bush, which can be found on open, dry sunny ground.

Juniper **is an old medicinal plant.**

ries were also chewed, or a liquid made from them was drunk as a safeguard against serious diseases. In fact the drinking of juniper spirit survived the days of the plague, and to this day juniper berries provide the English with gin, the French with genièvre, and the Germans with steinhäger.

It is also worth stressing that juniper really does have medicinal properties. The volatile (easily vaporized) oil from the berries was used as a diuretic. The berries also made a simple brew used as a folk medicine in Upper Bavaria against dropsy (a disease in which fluids collect in parts of the body). The power of this xerophytic (plants adapted to conditions in which there is a limited water supply) shrub of the sunlit slopes lies not only in its fruits but also in its wood, young branches, and root. Oil from the young wood used to be added to salves against rheumatism. Fragrant juniper resin was used instead of resin from the west Mediterranean which smells like incense when ignited, and which was one of the ingredients of the mixture used to mummify the dead.

Juniper wood is very firm, durable and delicately fragrant, and is therefore suitable for wood carving and for the inlaying of furniture. When a juniper implement was used for churning butter, it imparted an interesting, aromatic flavour. Juniper wood is used to this day for smoking and preparing meat.

There are a number of old superstitions connected with the varied uses of juniper. A walking stick made of juniper wood was said to safeguard pilgrims on their long journeys on foot. Its magical properties make juniper one of the most powerful plants against evil spirits. Smoke from juniper wood drives away serious illness, and also witches and devils. Not only can illnesses be driven away by

juniper, but with the chanting of a certain incantation they can be transferred to someone else — and let him get out of that!

There are also superstitions connected with the **Houseleek** (*Sempervivum tectorum*). In Europe, it is a plant of unusual appearance, calling to mind succulents (fleshy, moist plants) such as the cactus. Another similarity between these plants concerns the crowded fleshy leaves, forming a dense rosette, which is covered with a web. In some houseleeks (particularly those growing on sunbaked rocks or in dry places), this prevents the plant's valuable water content from evaporating.

In the past a particular favourite was **Roof houseleek** (*Sempervivum tectorum*) with its large green rosettes, the leaves tinged with red at the tips. They recalled the red beard of Jupiter, or Jove, the highest deity. This led to some houseleeks being called **Jove's**

Roof houseleek, once commonly used to protect houses from lightning.

used as a disinfectant. In 'plague houses' juniper berries were scattered onto the hot coals because the smoke was thought to drive away infectious diseases. The ber-

A **flowering** Roof houseleek, **with the rosettes of its offspring.**

house from bad luck. In the Middle Ages houseleek was also used as a protection against witches. It was hung in the chimney to safeguard against witches entering the house. It could also prophesy the future. If it bloomed with a red flower, there would be a joyful event. A white flower meant the death of someone in the house. Should the whole plant wither, the entire family would suffer great unhappiness.

The root of another plant, the hardy 'queen of the snow', also had magical power. Whoever carried it with him could be sure of eternal youth and protection against illness, especially dropsy. But to obtain the root of the **Christmas rose** (*Helleborus niger*) with its magical powers, it had to be dug from the earth in secret. Whoever sets out after the 'magic root' must drink, that morning, a glass of wine with garlic in it. This will ward off any headaches. He must also make a circle around the selected plant, using consecrated chalk, pray in the direction of the sun, after which he is allowed to sink his spade into the earth. But wait. While at work, he must not be seen by an eagle circling overhead, otherwise he will die within the year.

The large single flowers of the Christmas rose bloom so early that its name is appropriate. Compared with the blooms of other pre-spring flowers, the Christmas roses are unusually large, 3—7 cm (1—3 in) in diameter. However, the white or faintly pink petals of the flower are not part of the corolla, but the 5-sepalled calyx which looks like a corolla. The latter is not missing but has taken the shape of green, cone-shaped nectaries (glands) containing the sweet nectar. Beyond the nectaries are a quantity of filaments with round, lemon-yellow anthers. A number of ovaries in the centre of the flower ripen into seed folli-

beard. Jupiter ruled the world with the strength and power of violent lightning and loud thunder. For this reason, the plant connected with the god of thunder used to be planted on the highly inflammable thatched roofs of cottages and later on the top of walls near gates and on houses. The houseleek was supposed to prevent the house from being struck by lightning and set on fire. The species name *tec-*

torum comes from *tectum*, meaning roof. Mediaeval man placed enormous faith in such a small plant. It may only have been a superstition, but we too have our own. And some people still grow houseleeks on walls!

In Switzerland the houseleek was revered as a magical herb. We know, however, that the plant was not planted on the roof but on a stake in a fence to protect the

The hardy Christmas rose, **which was once highly regarded for its magical powers.**

a flower, a so-called biological flower.

The edelweiss, as the unsung queen of Alpine plant life, has always attracted the attention of mountaineers. As the tempting target for climbers and a favourite souvenir for tourists, it has become a popular Alpine symbol for many hotels, societies, mountain chalets and hunters. The flower

The 'flowers' of the Alpine Edelweiss are becoming so rare that the plant is now a protected species.

The Edelweiss — the emblem of the French National Park de la Vanoise.

cles (containers). The flowers of the Christmas rose bloom for a long time and do not mind snow drifts. The fruits ripen very slowly, the process being completed at the end of May or in June. By this time, the plant is covered in new, shining green leaves which are deeply toothed and last until the next flowering season.

The Christmas rose comes from southern Europe, and it is usually cultivated for its early spring flowers which brighten up gardens. In some places it grows wild.

Against Evil Spirits and Spell Binding

A legendary jewel among mountain flowers is the **Edelweiss** or **Lion's foot** (*Leontopodium alpinum*). This inaccessible flower grows high up, where the eagles live, on narrow ledges and tiny outcrops of steep limestone cliffs in the European and Asian mountains. Originally it also grew on Alpine meadows, but now there are none to be found in the Caucasus

or in the Urals. The plant naturally spreads up the mountain sides, from 1,600 — 3,400 m (5,250 to 11,160 ft) above sea-level in the Alps, but does not descend to the lowlands. When planted there by man, who wanted it to grow in his rock gardens, it completely changed. Originally low growing, it now became longer, while its woolly covering thinned out. In addition it turned green.

In the mountains the thick woolly covering protects the plant from the sudden changes of night and day temperatures, from water evaporation and from overheating. The thick growth of woolly hairs is filled with air pockets which reflect the rays of light with an enchanting silvery white glow. However, the 'flower' of edelweiss is afflicted with a most unpleasant change of appearance. This demonstrates to us that it is not a flower but a grouping of several tiny, globular collections of very small, yellowish flowers. Together with the supportive white woolly bracts they give the appearance of

image has also been used by artists.

This tough, hardy plant, growing at high altitudes, has even been described as being as strong as a lion. Its scientific name, in many languages, derives from the comparison of the flowering edelweiss to the image (*podion*) of a lion's (*leon*) foot. In the Dolomites, edelweiss is called *stella alpina*, meaning alpine star, because of an old legend which says it comes from the moon.

Herdsmen used smoke from burning edelweiss to drive away spirits from their cattle. They smoked out their cattle sheds to chase away evil powers.

Evil spirits are also chased away by the strong aroma of **Garlic** (*Allium sativum*). Bunches of garlic hanging under the eaves and near the door repulsed vampires. Some people used to wear garlic on a cord around their necks, or at the waist, because they believed it protected them against evil magic and the evil eye. Such a belief in the magic power of garlic dates back to antiquity. The ancient Egyptians placed garlic in the tombs of their dead — the remains of six garlic bulbs were found in the golden tomb of Pharaoh Tutankhamen (c. 1370—c. 1352 B.C.). However, poor people could only afford a clay model of garlic, painted white, on their graves.

The use of garlic is so varied and effective that its spread from country to country can surprise no one. As one of the oldest known medicinal herbs, garlic has left its traces not only in ancient Egypt, Greece and Rome, but also in the Orient and in China. Botanists, together with etymologists (people who study the history of words), have discovered that the Chinese knew garlic at the time of the first Chinese written characters (or letters of the alphabet), because one character represents its Chinese name — *suan*.

A string of garlic and a single clove, famous for its powerful flavour.

However, it is believed that garlic did not originate in China, but Siberia. From there it spread to the Mediterranean, to Sicily, and beyond.

Garlic is believed to improve both people's physical and mental strength. It fortified Roman soldiers before a battle, Greek athletes before a race, Syrian peasants at the time of harvest, and was chewed by the workers building

35

the pyramids, who needed every ounce of strength.

As the ancient scholar Pliny the Elder reports, garlic is a cure for colds, ulcers, snake bite, measles, and another 60 ailments and injuries. Garlic was also eagerly sought during dangerous outbreaks of cholera.

Recent research has justified many of these claims. It was proved in 1954 that garlic juice kills bacteria in only three minutes. Unfortunately, these excellent effects are accompanied by a strong smell which is released when the bulb is crushed, though it can be moderated by drinking milk. Garlic also contains a number of important minerals, including calcium, iron and iodine. It is used to relieve high blood pressure, hardening of the arteries, and heart and intestinal difficulties. It also protects people from infectious diseases. So while garlic has rid us of spirits and evil vampires, its campaign against illnesses goes on.

The Drops of the Alchemists

The plain and inconspicuously flowering **Lady's mantle** (*Alchemilla*) is, strange to say, a close relative of the beautiful rose. It has tiny, yellow-green flowers unlike the larger blooms of the rose. The common name derives from the palm-shaped leaves which are, when young, folded like a lady's mantle or cloak.

The historic importance of this plant can be understood from its scientific name, *Alchemilla*, which arose from a corruption of the Arabic word *alchymie*. Alchemists were the predecessors of chemists who attempted, from the 4th to the 17th centuries, to produce new substances. They worked with metals, dyes and drugs. The vision of immense wealth drove them to transform ordinary metals into precious ones, particularly gold.

Lady's mantle — the plant's name derives from the fact that the leaves are said to resemble a lady's cloak.

Their greatest desire was to produce the philosopher's stone — an imaginary stone, substance or chemical — which would make this possible. The rare ingredient they sought for this purpose was the natural 'heavenly' dew, which settled in the furrowed leaves of

The mysterious, long-forgotten signs used by alchemists, whose chief ambition was to turn metal into gold.

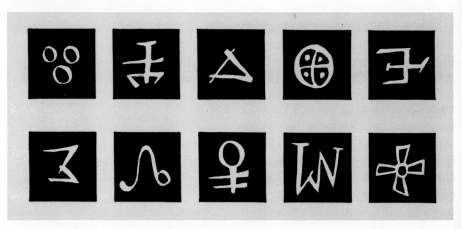

lady's mantle, like shining pearls. But they are not rain drops or dew. Pressure from the roots forces this moisture out through openings on the circumference of the leaves as surplus water. The tiny droplets roll down into the hollow in the centre of the leaf, and run together to form a 'magic' drop. This water was said to have supernatural power, which is why it was added to 'the elixir of life', a potion that it was hoped would keep people young for ever.

Even today people seek out lady's mantle in the meadows and on grassy spots, valuing the plant for its ability to cure inflammation, and heal nosebleeds and wounds.

Another plant used by the alchemists was the **Greater celandine** (*Chelidonium majus*). As frequently happens, the genus name of this herb conceals its early history. According to one version, the mediaeval interpretation of its name derives from the Latin *coelidonum* or *donum caeli*, meaning a gift from Heaven. It was believed that a plant with such a name and, in addition, full of peppery orange juice, must have supernatural powers. There was also a similarity to the human body because any part of the plant, apart from the seed, suffering an injury, wept droplets of 'golden-orange blood'. The juice was an important ingredient used by the alchemists when attempting to make the philosopher's stone, because it supplied the basic natural elements — air, earth, water, and fire.

The second and older version of its name also describes its magical power. The Latin name *Chelidonium* is derived from the Greek *chelidon*, meaning a swallow. The name therefore combines magical and healing powers because, according to Aristotle and Pliny the Elder, swallow parents seek out this plant for their young to give them keen sight. It was even believed that the plant would return

sight to those young birds that had gone blind in the nest. Another interpretation of the name connects the growth and withering of the plant with the arrival and departure of the swallows. But this only applies to certain parts of the world.

The species name *majus* means greater. This is a comparison with the **Lesser celandine** (*Ficaria ver-na*), which was called *Chelidonium minus* in the Middle Ages. It is a remote relation and is similar only in the strong yellow colour of the flowers.

Although the greater celandine contains strong, potentially poisonous chemicals, it was once used in folk medicine. Even today the juices are said to remove warts and freckles, and clear the skin of

When injured, the Greater celandine **'bleeds' a yellow juice.**

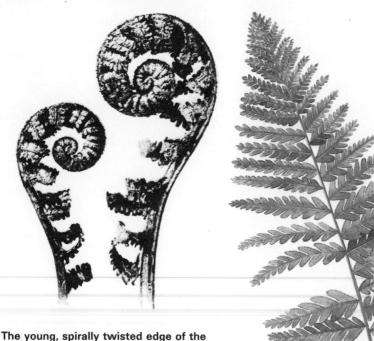

The young, spirally twisted edge of the leaf of the Male fern.

marks caused by the diseases psoriasis, herpes, and smallpox.

St. John's Eve

The **Male fern** (*Dryopteris filix-mas*), a well-known plant that grows in shady woods, has never been seen to flower. So does it actually do so? For a long time it was believed to flower just like any other plant, but in secret! Since no one has ever seen the fern flower, a superstition arose that it opens its golden flower only at midnight on the Eve of St. John or on Good Friday. Superstitious folk went out seeking the magic flower, but such a journey was only for the determined and brave. The flower was said to be guarded by evil spirits who used various apparitions to scare off the seekers. But the rewards were so great that many persisted; they believed that whoever obtained the flower would become invisible, immortal, and speak the language of animals and trees.

However if the flower was hard to discard, the root certainly was not. The root also had magic pro-

perties, and was worn next to the skin to guard against spells, devils and spirits. It could even bring success, particularly to hunters.

The more mysterious the plant is, the more superstitions surround it. The flower of the fern was not always thought to be golden. In some mountainous places, people sought a fern that had a fiery flower. An old legend says that this flower was the key to golden treasure.

Another plant connected with St. John's Eve is **St. John's wort** (*Hypericum perforatum*), which has attracted many superstitions and folk legends. The plant is not able for a quantity of dots on its leaves and flowers which gave the plant its species name. The spots are of two kinds. The translucent spots on the leaves are tiny reservoirs containing a bitter oil. The black spots on the edge of the leaves, on the golden-yellow corolla of the flower, on the calyx, the flower stalks and even on the seed capsules, are miniscule glands with a dark red content. If you crush a closed flower between your fingers, the red coloured substance is released, popularly called 'the blood of St. John'. However if you get it on your fingers, the skin becomes hypersensi-

Since the Male fern, *above,* neither flowers nor bears seed, it reproduces by means of spores. The absence of flowers once made people very superstitious about the plant, which was thought to have magical properties, particularly in its roots *(bottom).*

tive to light. Exposed to the sun, the skin reddens unpleasantly and blisters.

All organisms, especially albinos (lacking in normal colouring) are sensitive to sunlight after contact with St. John's wort. There is a story that describes what happened in the valley of the Euphrates and Tigris, 2,000 years before Christ. White sheep began to perish mysteriously on the fertile pastures of the green valley on the edge of the desert. The shepherds thought that the culprit was the local evil spirit. In order to outwit it, they used henna and tobacco leaves to colour all the sheep brown, thereby saving them. But then cows grazing pastures where St. John's wort grew began giving red milk! It was believed that a spell had been cast on these cows, and that they were giving blood and not milk. Legend has it that this magical plant originally grew from drops of blood from the head of John the Baptist.

The plant's scientific name recalls its glorious past in folk medicine. The Greek *hyper* means above, and *eikon* means image or a concept; combined, these words describe a plant of above average healing power. In the Middle Ages it was a miraculous, even universal medicine, perhaps throughout the whole of Europe. It was the best of all cures for both people and animals. Even today it is one of the medicinal herbs generally used in the home. It helps cure digestive problems, aids blood circulation, gives tranquil sleep, and also heals wounds, burns and hemorrhoids.

The plant has an equally good reputation for its magical properties. During the superstitious Middle Ages, fortunes were told according to its juices. It was a protection against lightning and drove out evil demons. Together with a certain incantation, it could even influence human willpower. St. John's wort gathered on the Eve

St. John's wort.

of St. John had the most magical effects. If a girl placed flowers of St. John's wort under her pillow, she would marry the man she was thinking of within the year.

Flowers of the Graveyard

One of the advantages of **Lesser periwinkle** (*Vinca minor*) are its tough, shining leaves which are not even harmed by frost. The leaves grow in pairs, opposite each other on thin stems, trailing on the ground to form a thick carpet in sparsely wooded areas. They are often used to cover the ground in shady gardens and in graveyards. The evergreen stems and garlands woven from them were used to adorn the dead at the time of Pliny the Elder, especially in winter when flowers were few. In Italy the custom was continued right up to the Middle Ages.

Periwinkle has also been associated with the dead in central and southern Europe. However, in eastern Europe it was a symbol of loyalty, replacing the myrtle used at weddings. In the Middle Ages periwinkle was considered to be a safeguard against charms and spells. It was also a protection against witches and incantations. Poachers had their superstitions, too. They used to go to the woods on St. John's Eve to gather periwinkle and wormwood (mugwort), but had to do so naked. Back at home, they boiled the magic plants with vinegar, and washed out the barrels of their guns with the brew so that they would not miss their aim.

The ancient Romans called periwinkle *pervinca*, but they used this term for other creeping plants as well. Some think that the scientific name *Vinca* is derived from the stems which are like strong twine

Flowers of the Graveyard (painting by J. Zrzavý).

(the Latin word *vincio* means to bind). Others believe it derives from the Latin *vinco*, meaning victory, because in remaining green for the whole year the plant achieves a victory over winter.

Strange Roots

There is an air of mystery for Europeans about **Ginseng** (*Panax quinseng*). In Eastern medicine, though, it is a valuable and most precious reality. For several thousand years it has been the most valuable medicinal herb and the king of all wild plants. According to legend, ginseng grows at a spot that has been struck by lightning, and therefore has the strength of heavenly fire. All the power of the plant is concentrated in the strange root which has the shape of the human body, which is why magical healing powers have been attributed to it. The root of ginseng is believed to have a miraculous effect on man's health, and his mental and physical alertness, giving him eternal youth. It has

The creeping stems of Lesser periwinkle **bearing flowers.**

40

a number of names, including 'the root of life' and 'the elixir of life'.

For a long time people believed in the supernatural origin of this ancient medicinal herb with magical qualities. They thought it to be the Holy Ghost, rising to his heavenly home from the underground root shaped in man's likeness. During his stay on earth he gives mankind his white blood for health and a long life. The oldest historical reports say that this mysterious plant was discovered and brought out from a deep cavern in China 5,000 years ago.

The all-healing ginseng is a perennial plant, approximately 50 cm (20 in) tall, with a whorl of several palm-shaped leaves divided into five parts. The tiny pinkish-white flowers bloom in July, but are replaced in September by ornamental fruit — red berries with white seeds. The strong fleshy root, having several side shoots, grows very slowly and is either gathered from the wild or grown specially for medicinal purposes.

Ginseng grows in damp soil in shady, mountain forests in Korea, China and the eastern part of the USSR. The interweaving of the branches of primaeval forests protects the plant from the rays of the sun and direct rainfall. The most valuable part of the plant is the root, well worth its weight in gold, which people hunt out in secret places in the mountains. It has the colour of carrots and a peppery taste.

Ginseng can also be cultivated in special plantations, given favourable soil and climatic conditions. The plant must be carefully nurtured for at least five to six years before the roots are gathered. An old oriental proverb says that ginseng only grows when it hears the footsteps of its cultivator. Experience shows that ginseng will not take root again on soil where it has previously grown for 10 years.

All the hard work that goes into

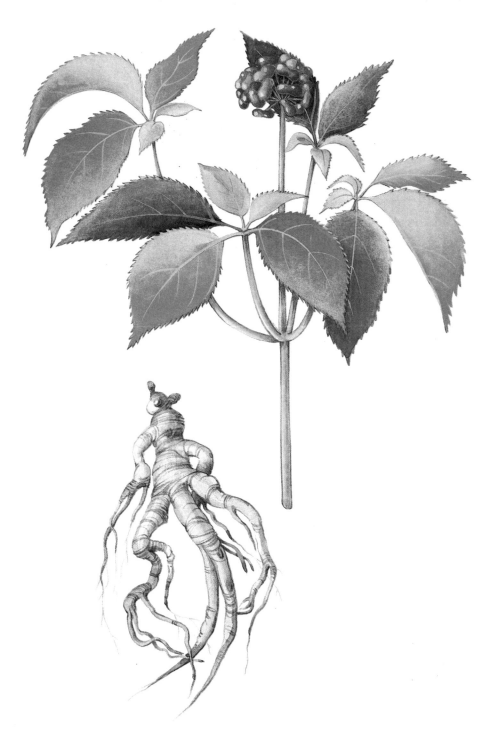

The fruit-bearing plant and root of Ginseng.

the cultivation of ginseng is counterbalanced by its tremendous curative powers. It has always been an exceptional all-purpose cure in eastern Asia. It cures both high and low blood pressure, anaemia, skin diseases, tuberculosis, defective memory, indigestion, and other ailments. Ginseng will also drive away fear, revive the tired and prolong life. Both the pharmaceutical and the cosmetic industries are eager for extracts from the ginseng root.

There are still many unclarified mysteries surrounding this magical plant. We do not know why the plant stops growing for a year if one of its leaves is damaged. And while we are aware of the curative

41

Cultivating Ginseng in North Korean plantations.

possibilities of ginseng, we do not know the composition or the value of the substances it contains. There is a strong belief that the root must be cut with a wooden knife in a clay pot. But we do not know why ginseng cannot be processed with metal instruments without losing its curative qualities.

A Chinese proverb of the first century B.C. summarizes the importance of this all-purpose cure. It reads: 'Ginseng lights up the eyes, encourages the spirit and deepens wisdom.'

Another root of a plant famous in the Middle Ages is the **Mandrake** (*Mandragora officinalis*), which is related to the nightshade family. The mandrake is branched in the likeness of the human body, and has its home in the Mediterranean region, especially in the mountains of Greece. The plant, with its rosette of large, curly leaves, is similar to sugar beet.

When it blooms, the whitish or blue-purple flowers sit in the furrow of the leaves.

The plant is renowned for its long, thick, beetlike root. In antiquity and the Middle Ages it was a drug shrouded in magic and superstitions. Its magical powers did not lie in the strongly toxic content of the plant but in the magical shape of the root. The rough likeness was improved by cutting away and shaping the image of the magical 'little man' (in German, *alraun*). It had the power to open treasure chests, make one invisible, bring good fortune, instil love, return lost strength, and to give protection against illness and evil spirits. It was often worn as a talisman (or lucky charm). It was also possible to tell fortunes with the mandrake, which is why it could be found in witches' kitchens, and was used by mediaeval magicians.

However, it was not at all easy

The Mandrake — note how its shape resembles the human body.

to get hold of the magic root. There are a number of instructions on how to locate it in writings from the Middle Ages. The mandrake was said to have its own special site. The magic plant grew only on places of execution, out of the body of a man unjustly executed. It was guarded by evil spirits who punished by death anyone who touched the plant with his hand. The root was therefore tied to the tail of a dog for him to pull it up. People had to block their ears with wax because the pulled root screamed and whoever heard the scream would die. The cleaned and adjusted root was looked after carefully, concealed in a valuable casket, washed on Sundays and saints days in wine, and dressed in silk garments. It was used in religious rites.

The shape of the root led the Greek philosopher and mathematician Pythagoras (c. 580—500 B.C.) to call the mandrake *planta semi-hominis*, meaning the semi-man plant, but the Persians called it the man-plant *merdun Giah.* The scientific name still used was derived, according to Theophrastus, from the superstition of Greek shepherds. They believed that the plant prevented their flocks from scattering and called it *mandra-ageiro*, meaning flock-hunter.

Where is the Treasure?

Are you planning an adventurous journey in search of treasure? If so, do not forget to take with you a magic guide — the **Common baneberry** (*Actaea spicata*). Such a suggestion might once have been found in a very old publication.

No one knows how this plant got involved with this superstition. Perhaps it is because it grows in the semi-darkness of damp, deciduous forests, and in deep abysses. It is also commonly found in beech woods. The evil smelling and perennial plant has a thick, brown-black root which was once used in folk medicine. The unremarkable small white flowers are crowded in clusters, and are later replaced by shiny black berries. They are also poisonous.

The large leaves, each with three serrated leaflets, are similar to the leaves of the **Elder** (*Sambucus nigra*), whose Greek name *aktaia* closely resembles *actaea*. Another explanation for the origin of the name comes from the Greek myth concerning Actaeon. This passionate young hunter wandered by chance into a forest cave, where the naked Artemis, goddess of the chase, was preparing to bathe. In punishment, she turned him into a stag, whereupon his own dogs chased and devoured him. *Spicatus*, meaning spike-shaped, refers to the arrangement of the flowers.

The German, French, Italian and other national names of the plant are derived from its old Latin name — *christophoriana*. This is a name closely connected with superstition. Long ago, the baneberry was

The symbols for the male and female Mandrake plants.

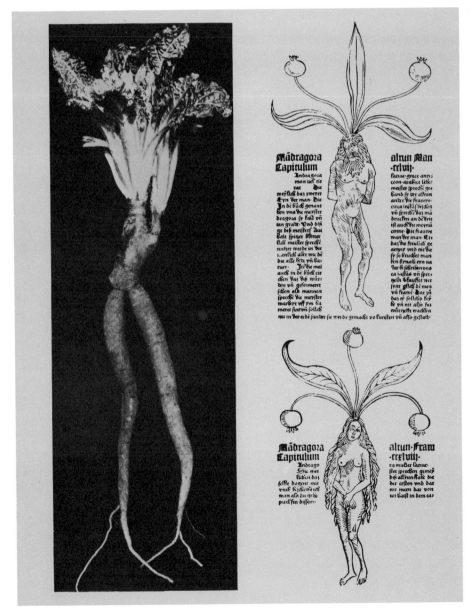

mental sight. The fruits are also remarkable, developing from the inconspicuous female flowers. The oval capsule, covered in soft (sometimes smooth) spines, has three compartments. When the fruit is ripe the capsule splits vertically, and the individual compartments separate with a snap from the central column. The ripe seeds, marbled like beans, are ejected for some distance. This ability to shoot its seeds some distance made some people think the castor-oil plant was magical. They said that where the seed fell, there 'treasure opened up'.

The seeds that are most poisonous, are also the most useful part of the plant. They contain a strong poison which is extracted from the plant's oil by the cold pressing method. The use of the oil as a laxative is generally known. It is also used in the cosmetic trade in producing mild soaps and hair oils. Another kind of castor oil is added to paints and wood preservatives. As its quality does not alter with changes in temperature, it is used for lubricating airplane motors. There is so much oil in the seed that 26—28 kgs (917—988 oz) are gained from 100 kgs (3,527 oz) of seeds. The main cultivators of the plant and producers of castor-oil are Brazil, India, Angola, and Mozambique.

The Castor-oil plant, **which grows in warm regions. On the** *left* **is a ripe, bursting seed pod, and on the** *right,* **its seed.**

Common baneberry, **which grows in the shade of deciduous forests.**

dedicated to St. Christopher, the patron saint of treasure seekers. With the help of the plant's magic and an incantation, a superstitious person was guided to the place where treasure was hidden.

In warmer regions, the **Castor-oil plant** (*Ricinus communis*) is regarded as the 'treasure seeker'. It is a plant that has long been cultivated, and is native of Africa where it is a perennial. It grows to a height of 13 m (43 ft). In warmer regions of the temperate zone of Europe it is grown as an annual industrial plant, 1.5—2 m (5—6.5 ft) high. Its sturdy growth, colourful stems, and particularly its large leaves with palm-shaped blades up to 1 m (3 ft) across, make the castor-oil plant a strikingly orna-

Native Magicians

Liberty caps (*Psilocybe*) are tiny, scaly mushrooms which you will easily overlook whether on damp grassland or on good quality wasteland. Many species grow in Australia and in New Guinea. They also grow in Europe, but have for long gone unnoticed.

On the other hand, the Mexican version, especially **Mexican liberty caps** (*Psilocybe mexicana*), have been used by natives from the time of the ancient Aztecs up to the present day. The Aztecs name for it has been preserved for the ritual mushroom *teonanacatl*, which means flesh of the gods. It is an essential part of the cult of the Mexican Indians, especially in the Oaxaca region. The magical mushrooms used to be collected by the Indians, when it rained, 1,000 years B.C. During the ceremony at which the witch-doctor presided, the mushroom was first of all invoked, and only then offered for eating as 'the body of god'.

Drugged by the magic mushroom, everyday reality changed for the Indians into wonderful experiences and colourful apparitions. A person under the influence of the mushroom seemed to step out of his body and enter another world. People who are ill with serious mental disorders have similar delusions. The substances of the mushroom have a similar effect to the substances contained in diseased rye seed. The magical hallucinogenic (delusion-inducing) poison of the mushroom was of interest to ethnographers (historians of human culture) and missionaries long ago, but the natives kept secret their knowledge of the sacred mushroom. That is why it did not become the object of scientific research until the present century. In the mid-fifties the American journalist R. Gordon Wasson brought back specimens of the mushroom, colour photographs of the area in which it grew, and his own experience from consuming the mushroom during a ceremony. The mushroom was reliably classified and described by R. Hein in Paris, and was chemically examined by A. Hofmann of Basle, Switzerland. It was discovered that the substance that affects the brain is the substance psilocybin, which gives its name to the plant.

Early botanists were not just scientists. They were also explorers who travelled to some of the world's most exotic and remotest regions in the search for unusual plant life.

The untouched forests of South America contain many mysterious plants.

Small fungi of the *Psilocybe* family:
(1) *Psilocybe zapotecorum*
(2) *Psilocybe aztecorum*
(3) *Psilocybe mexicana*.

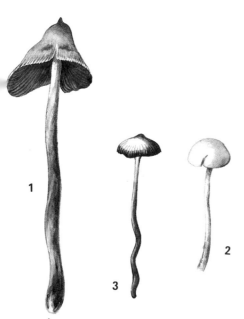

1

2

3

III BEWARE POISON!

Long ago people had already found out that some plants are extremely poisonous. However, in very small, correct doses, they can help cure the ill. So herbal poisons must be looked upon with the well-known saying in mind: 'There is some good in everything.' Most poisonous plants grow scattered over the tropical regions, but there are quite a few in Europe that we must be wary of.

Spring Flowers

The Latin name for the plant *Ranunculus acris* (**Meadow buttercup**), partly derives from the word *rana*, meaning frog. This may be because many buttercups grow near water and in damp areas, precisely where frogs live. The species name *acris*, which means acrid, indicates the toxic substance protoanemonin which is found in the meadow buttercup and throughout the whole *Ranunculaceae* family. The fierce, burning taste can affect pasture land where it grows and cattle avoid it. Yet it is not poisonous in hay. In earlier times it was believed that the buttercup was so poisonous it caused evil magic. A cow that lay on the plant was thought to have a bewitched udder.

The delicate, early spring **Wood anemone** (*Anemone nemorosa*) is also full of poison. The fresh sap of the plant contains a poison which causes blisters on sensitive skin. And as a herbal medicine it destroys bacteria and microscopic fungi. (Buttercups, the anemone and other related plants also contain healing chemicals.) The fresh plant has a bitter, corrosive taste as a protection against herbivores (plant-eating animals). However, the taste disappears when the plant is dried. This herb is also dangerous to man. It is said that anyone eating 30 plants could die, though it is not very likely anyone would consume such a large bunch of anemones. There is a greater likelihood that the plant might irritate the eyes of children who rub their eyes after picking the flowers.

Anemos is a Greek word meaning wind. Pliny believed the plant was so named because the flower blooms in early spring when the wind is strong, or perhaps because the delicate petals of the flower are scattered like snowflakes by the wind. (The flower of the wood anemone is not protected from the wind by leaves as it grows on a long stalk high above the three leaves.)

The **Lesser celandine** (*Ficaria verna*), previously called *Ranunculus ficaria*, is a plant containing several poisons. However the young leaves contain vitamin C and are not toxic, and are occasionally used in a spring salad. Nonetheless, there is a bitter, acrid flavour which even cattle on pastures avoid. Proof of the toxic quality of the lesser celandine is in the fact that the people living in the Alps and the Pyrenees in a bygone age dipped their arrows in its poisonous juices.

The lesser celandine frequently grows on damp soil in shady places. Its shining golden flowers do not bloom for long and achenes with seeds appear only rarely. The plant therefore spreads vegetatively. It forms root tubers underground and bulbils (small bulbs) in the axils of the leaves. The white bulbils in the leaf axils are propagating buds containing nourishing substances. They are carried away with the first flood water, and when they settle in suitable places grow into new plants. The plant is more frequently propagated in this way than through seeds.

The closed buds of the lesser celandine were once used as a substitute for the precious spice,

Poisonous plants grow in most countries, not only in more exotic climates, so be on your guard. It is hard to believe that these delicate European spring flowers, for instance, are poisonous, but they are. Those shown here are: **(1)** Lesser celandine — **the flowering plant with root tubers; after flowering, part of the stem bears leaf-axil bulbils (indicated by arrow); (2) White-flowering** Wood anemone **(3) Yellow-flowering** Buttercup **(4)** Meadow buttercup — **flowering plant and fruit.**

capers. The latter are the flower buds of the **Caper bush** (*Capparis spinosa*) which grows in the Mediterranean region, and they have a stimulating flavour which is lacking in the celandine buds.

The Soporific Perfume of Poison

The soporific, sweet perfume of the **Spurge olive** (*Daphne mezereum*) proclaims the arrival of spring. Although the scent attracts insects for pollination, there are few insects about between February and March when the plant is in bloom. That is why the plant has a strong perfume to tell the insects where they can find the pink flowers with their sweet nectaries. The flowers, in dense cylindrical spikes, cover the bare upper part of the stems. The leaves burst after the flowers wither, and are gathered in clusters at the end of the twigs. The wax-like, stiff flowers grow straight on the stem and have no corolla. Its role is taken by the calyx, which is shaped and coloured for this purpose.

The poisonous spurge olive looks quite different in the leafless woods of spring than in summer, when it is practically hidden beneath the dense undergrowth of beech woods, shady copses and damp, deciduous forests. It is betrayed only by its bright red berries, sitting directly on the twigs. The poisonous stone-fruit develops at the beginning of each summer from the fertilized ovaries of the flowers.

The white flowering spurge olive has yellow fruit which is eaten by the birds, who are not affected by the plant's poison. They pluck the bright berries and carry the indigestible seeds with their droppings to places where they eventually take root. However, the plant's poisons will make any animal that eats it ill.

The ancient Greeks and Romans

Spurge olive **blooms early in the spring in sunlit woods.**

used spurge olive as a medicinal herb for various ailments. The bark and the seeds were used in folk medicine as poultices (healing ointment on a muslin bandage) to ease pain. Yet it appears that this ancient remedy still has much to offer. Recent scientific reports suggest that one of its chemicals might help treat leukemia.

The scientific name for spurge olive — *Daphne* — is based on an ancient Greek myth. Apollo, the

god of the sun, fell in love with the lovely nymph Daphne. To escape from his advances, she begged protection from Zeus, who changed the girl into the tree *Laurus nobilis*, as its original name had been *Daphne*. Because of the similarity of the leaves between this tree and the spurge olive, Linné renamed the latter *Daphne*, for it seemed more appropriate to the myth about the charming bush which shows its loveliness early in spring and then, for the rest of the year, is concealed beneath the branches of trees.

Nature Heals

The **Common foxglove** (*Digitalis purpurea*) is one of the strikingly ornamental plants of the country-

The Common foxglove, a striking plant which provides a useful drug.

side. It was brought to central Europe from the light forests of southern and western Europe by man, who discovered a splendid remedy in its handsome flower. It is a real queen among medicinal herbs because its toxic chemicals are effective in treating the heart and nerves. But care must be taken and the drug used only by physicians. An overdose means death.

The healing drug is obtained from the rosette of basal leaves which forms in the plant's first year. In the second year, a 1 m (3 ft) stem, or longer, grows from its centre with a spike of large, downward turned flowers along one side. The lower lip of the corolla is decorated with dark spots and a light rim. The common foxglove is not always purple in colour. Darker and lighter specimens, and even white flowers, are often found.

The foxglove is often grown in gardens as an ornamental flower, or in larger quantities for the needs of the pharmaceutical industry. More frequently grown for medicinal purposes is a relative, *Digitalis lanata*, which comes from the Balkans. It is a warmth-loving plant and has a much higher content of the substances required. The quantity of such chemicals is directly dependent on the intensity of photosynthesis (the process by which plants convert sunlight into energy). Therefore, the effective substances are mostly in the leaves (where this process occurs), and in the afternoon when the sun is at its hottest. At night, the chemicals are broken down and transferred to another part of the plant.

Common foxglove has a long history as a medicinal herb. It was used in folk treatment in Ireland in the 5th century, in the rest of Europe from the 11th century, and it was introduced into orthodox medicine by William Withering around 1775.

Nature has concealed very valuable healing substances in such unattractive forms as **ergot** (a rye disease, caused by fungus). In large doses ergot is poisonous. As a drug it regulates the contraction of the arteries and stops the internal bleeding of some organs.

Ergot is artificially cultivated as an important raw material for the pharmaceutical industry. Selected species of rye are inoculated with a substance containing the germs of ergot with the aid of a specially adjusted machine. It passes through the field of grain, while its needles puncture the ears and spray them with the special substance. The collecting of ergot at the end of July is also done by machine. More than 0.5 tons of ergot can be obtained from 10,000 sq m (1 hectare).

The ergot that falls into the soil during harvesting can survive the winter, thanks to its rich supplies of carbohydrates and fats.

Ergot has been a danger to mankind on many occasions. There is a case recorded at Limoges in France where, in the year 944, a total of 40,000 people lost their lives. For a long time the cause of death was unknown and was ascribed to an epidemic. Determining the cause was hampered by the fact that the illness lasted a long time. Epidemics of the same kind, from an unrecognized cause, occurred several more times until, in 1630, the French doctor Thuillier conducted an experiment proving that the cause of death was ergot. When ergot is milled with unclean grain into flour, it produces chronic poisoning, known as ergotism.

The curative uses of ergot were known to the Chinese, the Assyrians, and the Persians before the birth of Christ. In Italy, on the other hand, it was said that an extraction of ergot was part of the infamous poisoning of the Borgias.

Lily of the valley (*Convallaria*

Ears of rye are inoculated with the germs of ergot at the time of flowering. Later, small purple fruits form on the spiked ergot *(right)*.

majalis) is so toxic that it even poisons the water in a vase in which a bunch of flowers has stood overnight. The creeping rhizome, the broad lance-shaped leaves whose lower part forms a sheath, the strongly fragrant flowers with their round, bell-shaped corollas, as well as the fruits (round red berries) are all poisonous. Yet the entire plant can also be used as a curative drug, but only under strict medical supervision. Just like the substances in foxglove, those in lily of the valley can attack the heart.

Lily of the valley has other uses. Its dried flowers are crushed and added to snuff. And the aromatic, essential oil is used in perfume and skin lotions.

Lily of the valley is a beautiful plant, particularly in sunlit woods,

copses and hedgerows, not only in Europe, but also in North America and in the moderate northern parts of Asia — Japan and China. It often grows in large groups so that some spots are completely covered with the strong fragrance of the flowers which carries for long distances. There are some countries where it is valued so highly that it is even protected by law. They include Austria, Switzerland, and both West and East Germany.

The lily of the valley can easily be grown in gardens and is a suitable plant for forcing into early growth, so that we can enjoy its flowers in the winter and early spring. Linné named the flower *Convallaria* in 1737, and for one species added the name *majalis*, meaning May. Thus he changed its

earlier recognized name *Lilium convallium*, meaning lily of the valley, but that is what it is still called by the English, French (*Lis des vallées*), Italians (*Giglio delle convalli*) and the Dutch (*Lelietje-van-dalen*). The name *Convallaria* combines the Latin *convallis* (valley) and the Greek *leirion* (lily).

The Biblical Lily

The **Crown imperial** (*Fritillaria imperialis*) is botanical proof of the proverb 'pride goes before a fall'. According to ancient legend the imperial lily was a very noble, and perhaps the most beautiful flower in the Garden of Eden. It was so proud of its beauty that it looked down on the other flowers which looked up to it with quiet humility and respect. But when God saw it,

50

Lily of the valley — **fragrant but poisonous.**

its appearance but also for its strong odour. The entire plant smells, but in particular the yellowish bulb which lacks a protective skin. Although the plant also contains a poison, the starchy bulbs are sometimes eaten because they lose their toxicity when cooked.

The imperial lily has won a permanent position among the ornamental flowers of the spring garden. It originated in Persia, Afghanistan and the western Himalayas. From Persia it was first taken to Palestine, and later attracted the eager interest of the Turks in Constantinople. Within a few years it was in the royal gardens in Vienna. By the end of the 16th century it had rapidly spread through European gardens. At first it was a fashionable flower, but it later spread to humbler country gardens, being known as the 'Imperial or Royal Crown', as older botanists first called it (*Corona imperialis*).

The imperial lily, a close relative of true lilies, was a popular flower in Palestine even in biblical times, when it was depicted on coins. And apparently it was the evangelic lily which was so majestical that even King Solomon in all his glory could not match it.

All Mushrooms Can be Eaten, But Some Only Once

Of the three poisonous toadstools the sinister beauty is the **Fly agaric** (*Amanita muscaria*). It is known practically all over the world, probably growing in every forest in the northern hemisphere and in some places in the southern hemisphere. It has a bright red cap extravagantly set with white scabs. When the fungus develops during dry weather the scabs are thicker and irregular, and are easily washed away by rain. When young, the whole fruit body is concealed in a white veil which tears

he punished the lily's pride by turning the upward-held flowers downwards, towards earth. From then on, the lily, with its drooping flowers, is constantly weeping over its guilt. Teardrops can be found each morning in the bell-shaped flower. That is how legend and Shakespeare, years later, described it.

The botanist has a different explanation. The drooping of the flower protects the large, globular nectaries which are inside on the lower part of every petal, and exude an attractive nectar for insects. The large flowers are coloured from red to orange, and even yellow. They are born four to six in a ring at the top of a tall, sturdy stem, with an exotic tuft of green leaves above them. The whole plant has a regal appearance. It is exceptional, not only for as the fungus grows. Fragments remain on the cap and in a few concentrated rings on the bottom of the stipe, instead of on the sheath as is usually the case with the *Amanitae*. There is a white ring on the upper part of the stipe (or stalk).

With time, views on the degree of toxicity of the fly agaric have changed. Once it was taken to represent all poisonous toadstools and was the symbol of evil in fairy tales. Yet later it proved that, though being poisonous, it is not always fatally so. It contains chemicals which have a narcotic effect on the nervous system. Some

northern nations have used this aspect in religious ceremonies. The poison also has an intoxicating effect on animals. Squirrels, who like to nibble various fungi, behave drunkenly, and flies drop to the ground. Apparently one ancient recipe involved sprinkling a fly agaric cap with sugar, or brewing one with sugar, and giving it to the flies to kill them. This ancient recipe can be deduced from the Latin species name of the plant *muscaria*, meaning flies.

The two toadstools which have been best researched are the fly agaric and the **Death cap** (*Amanita phalloides*). The latter presents

real danger for the inexperienced gatherer of fungi. It is an inconspicuous toadstool but deadly poisonous! Neither its shape nor colour attract attention, and it is said that its taste is not warningly unpleasant, either. One person made a dreadful mistake and ate it, but with great good fortune and the assistance of doctors survived. He thought that he had been collecting ordinary edible mushrooms!

Some idea of the strength of the death cap's poison is given by the following example. Sufficient poison to cover the point of a knife (a mere 0.5 gr) will kill 100,000 mice which, when laid side by side, would make a line 18 km (11 miles) long. This deadly poisonous toadstool contains three groups of poisons of various strength and differing effect, the most dangerous of which destroys liver cells. First aid and treatment is all the more difficult because signs of poisoning do not appear immediately, but 8—12 hours after consumption, when the food has been digested.

Death cap grows mainly in warm regions under oak and beech trees from July to September. The young toadstools grow from the oval covering of the veil which resembles the shell of an egg. As the toadstool pushes through, the covering is torn and fragments of it remain at the base of the stipe as the typical 'chalice of death'. None of its possible doubles has this chalice!

Coming across **Devil's boletus** (*Boletus satanas*) is a thrilling and increasingly rare experience on an

Crown imperial, **originally grown in Asia, but for the past 400 years a great European favourite.**

The handsome, spotted Fly agaric **(1) was earlier taken to represent all poisonous fungi. However, we now know that the Death cap (2) is far more dangerous. It is also much more easily found than** Devil's boletus **(3), which can be located, if you search hard enough, in grassy forest areas.**

excursion into the forest. It grows in grassy areas, open to the warming rays of the sun, and is found in the warmer parts of the temperate zone of the northern hemisphere. The colour of the thick stipe accords with the purplish-crimson colour attributed to the devil. Linguists tell us that the name derives from the Hebrew word *shatan*, meaning opponent or plaintiff.

The more highly coloured devil's boletus is less dangerous than death cap. Poisoning is not fatal but will cause violent sickness. It is even claimed that heat causes the toxic substances to disintegrate. Although its fleshy appearance is an inducement to collecting this mushroom, its place is among the poisonous fungi and not the edible ones.

How Old is the Yew Tree?

The **Yew** (*Taxus baccata*) has a sombre, almost gloomy impact on people. It is not until the autumn that its dark green, flat leaves are enlivened by the red, cup-shaped arils bearing the seed. The sweetish, fleshy cup is the only non-toxic part of the tree which contains a deadly poison.

The popular use of yew wood as a valuable raw material for ornamental wood-carving and for turning has led to its disappearance from the countryside. The few remaining trees, often of venerable age, are protected in many places as natural monuments. However, it seems that estimates of 1,000—2,000 years are somewhat exaggerated. According to probes made into the wood of the trunks, we can put the age of the oldest yew trees at 400—600 years (the large number of annual rings · is sometimes the result of several close trunks fusing together).

Primaeval man used yew to make his primitive tools. Bows, knives and combs have been found in dwelling places in Switzerland and Austria. Later, the yew tree was intentionally removed from pastureland so that cattle would not be poisoned. It has been said that young horses, who nibbled at the new shoots, fell dead on the spot. It is not therefore surprising that such an effective poison was used by primitive peoples — the ancient Gauls and the North American Indians — as a poison for their arrows. In mediaeval superstitions, the effect of the poison was magnified even more. It was said that whoever

Yew trees are such valuable sources of wood that few are left. If you do find one try to estimate its age. The oldest known yews are 600 years old.

The fruiting twig of the Yew on an illustration by Matthioli, 1562.

Tis.   Taxus.   Eibenbaum.

falls asleep under a yew tree will die. So it became the symbol of sorrow and death.

At the present time, more and more yews are being planted in parks and in the residential districts of large cities. They are a welcome accompaniment to the remnants of old yews found by cliffs and in mixed woods.

Poison on the Fields and in Water

The **Corn cockle** (*Agrostemma githago*) is one of those plants that have been man's companions for a very long time. It has kept pace with the rhythm of field work and has followed the cultivation of cereals throughout the temperate zone of the world. Originally a species (*Agrostemma gracile*) from the near east steppes, it is now regarded exclusively as a field weed. Even scientifically the silky-grey, hairy plant with purplish-red flowers has been given a name designating it an ornament of the field, a bright garland found round fields of grain (deriving from the Greek *agros* meaning field, and *stemma* garland). But farmers do not value it so highly. Several hundred poisonous seeds mature on a single plant. The ripe seed capsules open by folding back to allow the seeds to fall out. Many years ago the seeds got into the flour milled from uncleaned grain. The blue-tinted flour had a bitter taste and was a danger to the lives of both people and domestic animals. The poison causes the red corpuscles in the blood to disintegrate. Fortunately, thanks to modern farming methods, the poisonous weed has now disappeared from most fields.

It is a known fact that the hundreds of different plants in the carrot family *Daucaceae* are very difficult to tell apart. This is also true of one of the most dangerous carrots — **Cowbane** (*Cicuta virosa*). It is sturdy, grows up to 1 m (3 ft)

The poisonous Corn cockle, **once a widespread field weed, is fast disappearing due to modern farming methods.**

high, and has a pleasant carroty smell and sweetish taste. The leafy, hollow stem grows from a fleshy and hollow rootstock. The surface of the rootstock is ridged in circles and divided inside into regular partitions and hollows. Yet such a sturdy cowbane can be unpleasantly deceptive, pretending to be a well-grown celery. This has been the downfall of quite a few children who, like little Robinson Crusoes, were trying to prepare a meal from what they could find in the wild. Most of the plant's

poison is in the rootstock at the time when flowering occurs. The poison can also seep into water, for instance a well, near where cowbane is growing.

The Death Sentence

The **Hemlock** (*Conium maculatum*) has been infamous as a poisonous plant since the time of the ancient Greeks. The entire plant is toxic, but the most strongly poisonous part is the fruit — lengthwise-ridged seeds. Some peoples

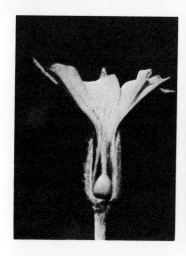

Development of the Corn cockle **flower after pollination and fertilization.**

The sturdy Cowbane **and, on the** *left,* **a cross-section of its root.**

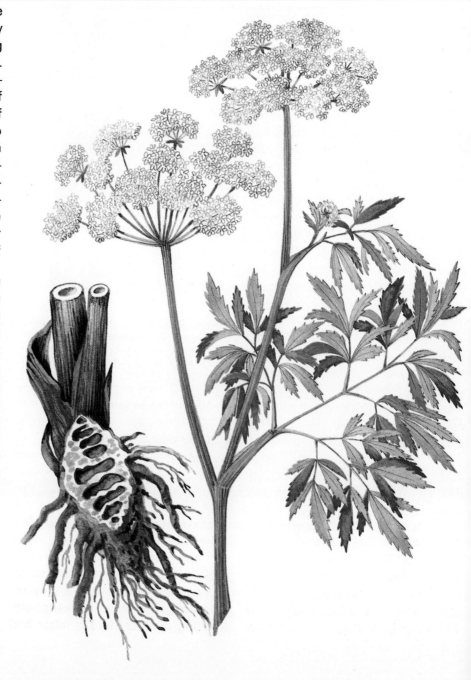

dried and used them to relieve pain. However, wrongly used, they had the opposite effect, causing a dull headache or even poisoning. The first symptom is a tingling, followed by a loss of movement of the limbs, complete paralysis of the body, and finally an inability to breathe and heart failure. Death occurs with the victim fully conscious. The strong poison in hemlock has a similar effect to the poison strychnine. It was used by the ancient Greeks to execute their victims. To reduce pain the juice of poppy was added to the poison.

In the 5th century A.D. a cup of hemlock poison was the means of legal execution in Athens. A cup of the poison ended the life of the famous Greek philosopher Socrates (c. 470—399 B.C.), who was condemned to death for his ideas. His loyal pupils and friends were present at his death. For as long as he could, he recounted his sensations and the exact course and action of the poison to his pupil Plato (c. 428—348 B.C.), who wrote them down.

An Arrow Kills in Silence

It is a vegetable juice which kills so silently that no one knows whence the arrow flew.
(Humboldt and Bonpland, 1880)

The mysterious curare, a poison despatched to its victim on the point of an arrow, is death carrying. (It can, however, also be used in medical clinics to alleviate some forms of muscular paralysis.) The primitive weapon comprises a blowing tube and a bamboo quiver to hold the arrows. The arrows are made from the ribs of palm leaves. The point of the arrow is dipped into curare poison which shows as a dark spot. The blow tube is over 2 m (6.5 ft) long, into which the Indian places a light arrow. He then takes a deep breath and suddenly blows out the arrow. When the victim is struck, death is certain and agonizing in full consciousness. However, curare only kills when it gets into the blood stream. It causes paralysis of all muscles and the nervous system. The muscles for breathing also cease to function and the victim dies of suffocation.

It is remarkable that a poison so infamously dangerous can also cure people. If swallowed in small doses it will relieve stomach troubles. Nothing bad can happen provided there is no open wound in the mouth through which the drug, and therefore also the poison, can get into the blood circulation.

The poison called curare is contained in some tropical woody vines. Its composition differs according to region, and from tribe to tribe. It is a mixture of around 30 components. Many of the vines belong to the genus *Strychnos*. The South American species of *Strychnos toxifera* and others have highly poisonous chemicals

Hemlock, **with a detail of its flower and fruit on the** *left.*

from the group of curarines. The bark is scraped from large vines, and is then ground, mixed with cold water, and strained through a fibrous material into a clay receptacle. The liquid thickens with heating until its taste is bitter and

it looks like tar. The Indians always use fresh plants to prepare their poison, which can be stored for a long time, up to several decades.

Asian species of *Strychnos* from Ceylon, India, and other tropical regions, also contain highly toxic

The ancient Greek philosopher Socrates, with a group of his followers.

spurges. The poison will kill an animal by inducing heart failure. However, the poison will not effect the flesh, which can be eaten.

There are several species of *Strophanthus* growing in central and eastern Africa. In western tropical Africa we find *Strophanthus gratus*. Its seeds are the raw material for the production of drugs containing ouabain, which has a similar effect on the heart as digitalis.

Golden Helmet

Monkshoods are plants that are ornamental though highly poisonous. The most poisonous of all is **Solomon's monkshood** (*Aconitum napellus*), containing the chemical aconitine which is one of the strongest and most rapidly acting poisons used in folk medicine. The most toxic part of the plant is the young rhizome which provides a curative drug. The poison content of the rhizome fluctuates, being highest in winter and lowest in summer. Just a few grammes of the rhizome are fatal, causing paralysis of the central nervous system.

The toxic properties of another species, *Aconitum lycoctonum*, must not be underestimated although it contains no aconitine. An indication of just how poisonous it is can be found in its species name, coming from the Greek

chemicals. In the Indo-Australian regions there is a tree called *Strychnos nux-vomica*. The white flowers are followed by large yellow-orange berries, like apricots. Inside, there are 8—12 round, flat seeds, like buttons. Their surface is slightly furry. The highly toxic drug contains the poisonous substances strychnine and brucine. It does not contain curarine, and neither do the Asian and African species from the Philippines, Java and tropical Africa. The strong poison is a curative drug, provided it is given in small doses under medical supervision, though it is not used very much now. On the other hand, it is still an effective substance for destroying rats.

Other plant families contribute their vegetable poisons to the arrow poison. They include *Meni-*

spermaceae and the plant *Chondodendron tomentosum*. This is a climbing vine with heart-shaped leaves. The Peruvian Indians call the bunches of purple fruits *ampihuasca*.

Natives in Africa also use arrows with poisoned tips when hunting. They seek the poisons in the tropical jungle, hunting out the *Strophanthus* plant which is difficult to get at. It is the vegetable arrow poison of the Old World. The poison is obtained from the seeds of the plant, when it has shed its long feathery covering of hairs. The poisonous liquid in which the arrow heads are dipped is thick like honey. To increase its effect, various ingredients are added, such as an extract from the roots of the plant, or from banana flowers, or the juice from the fleshy cactus-like

Curare is a death-dealing poison applied ▶ to the tip of an arrow before being fired at a victim. The poison is found in tropical vines, its composition varying from region to region, and from tribe to tribe. Illustrated here are **(1)** A characteristic Indian weapon, the blow tube and a bamboo quiver **(2)** The poisonous plant *Strychnos toxifera* **(3)** A native making arrows poisoned with curare **(4)** *Strophanthus* **(5)** A map showing the distribution of the arrow-head poison curare in South America **(6)** Seeds of *Strychnos nux-vomica*.

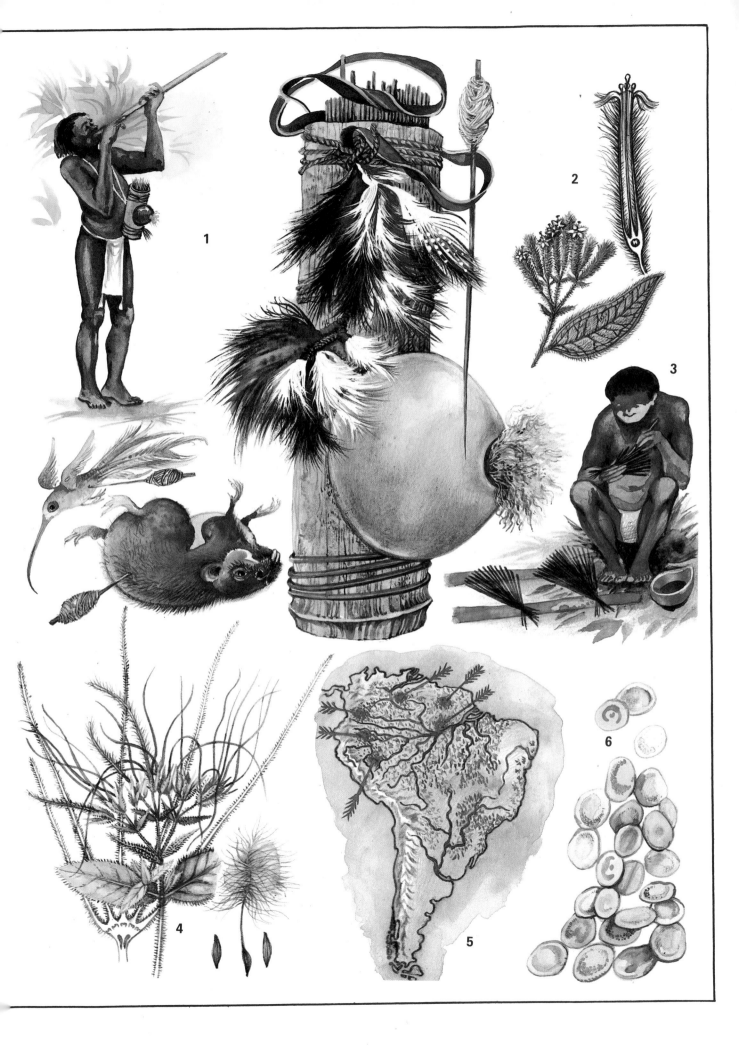

has also passed into some of the common names of monkshood.

The local name of the blue-flowering **Solomon's monkshood** (*Aconitum napellus*) reflects the shape of the flower which is curved like a hood. The golden flowers of wolf's bane are hairy and have a cylindrical helmet extended towards the back. For this reason, the flowers can be pollinated only by bumble bees with their long proboscis (tube-like organ). The fruits are smooth arils (exterior coverings) contain-ing a quantity of black seeds.

In his *Metamorphoses* Ovid reveals the origin of monkshood. Apparently, the dangerous plant arose from the poisonous spittle of the three-headed guardian of the entrance to the underworld, the legendary dog Cerberus. There is also a Christian legend which explains that God created flowers for people's pleasure, but the Devil looked on some of them with the evil eye and they became poisonous.

Monkshood was used by Me-

The flowers of the sturdy White hellebore are arranged in rich panicles.

The yellow-flowering Monkshood **and the blue flower of** Solomon's monkshood.

lykos meaning wolf, and *kteino* meaning kill, or the Latin name *vulparia*, from *vulpes*, meaning fox. The Greek physician Dioscorides (c. 40—90 A.D.) wrote that the monkshood was used for poisoning wolves (and also foxes): 'For this purpose its black root is put into raw meat which these animals consume and then die.' The ancient Gauls and Germans, too, hunted animals of prey with spears, the points of which had been dipped in the poisonous juice of monkshood. This ancient use dea, the renowned sorceress and poisoner who wanted to kill Theseus, one of the greatest heroes of Greek myths. Also, in the Middle Ages monkshood was one of the herbs used in preparing magic remedies.

Solomon's monkshood grows in Europe and Asia in damp places, while wolf's bane grows only in central and southern Europe. Both species grow at high altitudes. Since the Middle Ages, they have been grown in gardens, first as a medicinal herb and magical plant, later as a vigorous, ornamental plant.

Sneezing Powder

In central and southern Europe **White hellebore** (*Veratrum album*) grows on damp mountain meadows. It is a sturdy plant about 1.5 m (5 ft) high. The broadly oval and pleated leaves of hellebore are extremely attractive. They grow singly, scattered around, or in groups in the dwarf pine zone, right up to the snow mark.

White hellebore is listed amongst the medicinal herbs. The drug is in the strongly poisonous rootstock which is dug out of the ground in the autumn. It is mainly used in veterinary medicine or for the extermination of insects, and destroys fleas, lice and other insects. Powder made from the root, or even the unpleasant smell of the dense flower arrangement is

White hellebore **on a mountain meadow.**

an irritant, causing sneezing. This aspect has contributed to some of the plant's names. Another name derives from a likeness between its greenish flowers and those of the Christmas rose.

White hellebore contains many chemicals, some of which are especially toxic for horses and cattle, goats, sheep, fowl, and also dogs and cats. Because the plant is also bitter, older animals avoid it, but since young sheep nibble at most plants they sometimes get poisoned. Hellebore is particularly dangerous in hay because it does not

lose its poisonous properties when dried.

Given this information, it is strange to report that sheep on a mountain meadow in the Tatra Mountains consumed white hellebore — and nothing happened! Both the sheep and the people who consumed products made from the sheep's milk showed no signs of poisoning. What is the explanation? It seems likely that the plant's ability to poison depends on when the plant grows, on the weather, and on the resistance of the animals.

IV GLOBE TROTTERS

Man has had far-reaching affects on the natural and original areas where plants grow. He has purposely selected some plants to transfer elsewhere and cultivate. Others naturally followed man as the unwanted accompaniment of human settlements, and undesired weeds of the field. Plants also quickly spread to pieces of land which man left vacant.

Among the plants that have spread the most are what we call weeds. They grow wherever there are crops and compete with them for sunlight, water, and also for space for their roots. They grab from the soil large quantities of nutrients intended for the cultivated plants and thus reduce the harvest.

Both the Old and New Worlds have exchanged many plant species. For instance, the European plantain spread to America where the Indians called it 'the trail of the white man' because lambs' tongue plantain, in particular, with its broad leaves, covers the soil of worn paths. In return, the American chamomile has spread to Europe.

Out into the World in 10-League Boots

The annual garden plant and field weed **Gallant soldier** (*Galinsoga parviflora*) has its home in the Peruvian Andes. From South America it has spread fairly recently to the whole world. At the end of the 18th century it was first cultivated as a new, unknown plant in the botanical gardens in Madrid, and

The dispersion of the potato, rubber tree **and** Foreign willow herb. **While the** Foreign willow herb **spread by itself, the** potato **and the** rubber tree **were helped by man.**

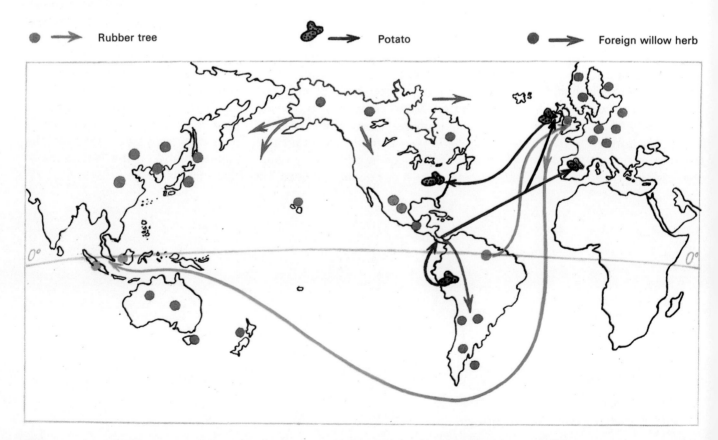

Rubber tree   Potato   Foreign willow herb

The **weed** Gallant soldier, **commonly found in gardens and fields.**

plants growing from the mature, scattered seeds. Originally from the tropics, the plant's seeds are not sensitive to damp or cold, nor do they lose their ability to germinate for many years. A single, smallish plant forms several thousand flower heads, each producing almost 40 fruits. So, under favourable conditions, up to 150,000 seeds will mature. They germinate only a few days after maturing, and the plant flowers from 6 to 8 weeks after germinating!

The small capitula imitating flowers have a yellow centre surrounded by an insignificant ray of white, tongue-shaped flowers. The capitula are slightly smaller than those of a relation, the **Hirsute gallant soldier** (*Galinsoga hirsuta*), which has a projecting white hairy stem.

The **Foreign willow herb** (*Epilobium adenocaulon*) has spread through the world with extreme rapidity from North America. It most likely first appeared in Europe in the 1880s in England. From here it spread north, east and south, not

then in 1810 in Berlin as a novelty. The manager of the Madrid botanical gardens was the physician, Martinez Galinsoga, whose name was given to the new plant by the botanist Antonio José Cavanilles.

A moderately tall plant with a smooth, fleshy stem, it rapidly ran wild from gardens to wasteland and rubbish heaps. It also spread among crops in the fields and vineyards, as well as among the ornamental flowers and vegetables in gardens. There is always a continuous supply of young

Foreign willow herb **and, on the** *right,* **its seed with down.**

being found in central Europe until the 1950s and 1960s. It has taken its place so perfectly among local flowers that it grows not only on rubbish heaps and wasteland, but can also be found along forest paths, at the sides of meadows and springs, and on damp pasture land. It seeks out damp and shady spots at lower altitudes.

The small, dark pink flowers appear on the plant from July to September. Almost at once they transform into long narrow pods full of light seeds. There are about 170 seeds in one pod, and one plant forms 60—80 pods, though 200 have been known. The immense quantity of 10—14,000 seeds, each with a tuft of down, are easily distributed by the slightest breeze over great distances. What is more, the lids of the capsules open only slowly, so the seeds leave the mother plant in stages, over several days.

This highly effective manner of spreading enables the willow herb, one of 180 species of the large *Epilobium* genus, to occupy and conquer ever new, often remote territories. The strange way in which some plants spread is illustrated by **Canadian fleabane** (*Erigeron canadensis*). Just like willow herb this rush, or Canadian water weed, came to Europe from North America.

The seed capsules of fleabane can be carried on the wind as they are equipped with a very fine, dirty white down. Back in the 17th century the down was used by taxidermists to stuff birds. But in 1655 a specimen was taken from Canada to Paris, where the stuffing was probably damaged or changed. The seeds contained in the down were released, and gradually spread through the Old World. The fleabane found a new habitat in Europe and became a customary field weed and a garden weed on drier soils.

The genus name of fleabane is

connected with its down. *Erigeron* is a combination of the Greek *eri*, meaning soon, and *géron*, meaning old man — in the sense that the white down, as a sign of old age, appears very soon after flowering.

Canadian fleabane **and, on the** *right* **an enlarged flower head.**

The small-flowered **Touch-me-not** (*Impatiens parviflora*) is spreading to Europe and North America from Central Asia, Mongolia and Turkestan. According to older reports, it was first brought from Mongolia to Berlin in the first half of the last century. Before long touch-me-not had spread to the city outskirts and beyond. It seeks out damp spots in forests, gardens and parks. On dry, crumbling soils, rich in nutrients, it covers whole areas. The small yellow flowers have a straight, pointed spur. They are not as attractive as the more sturdy *Impatiens noli-tangoro*.

By Water, Quickly and Easily

A Canadian immigrant in Europe is the **Canadian water weed** (*Elodea canadensis*), which earned its name from its astonishing propagating ability. This ability is so immense that the plant is capable of

Canadian water weed — **it looks small and harmless, but in fact can propagate at a furious speed, quickly 'strangling' ponds.**

The small flowers of Touch-me-not.

taking over and filling up pools, dead stretches of rivers, and ditches. It does not spread through seeds but by segments of its dense leafy stems. In Europe, the Canadian water weed is directly dependent on vegetative propagation. It is a dioecious plant (one plant has the male organ, another the female organ). However, only the female plant has gone out into the world while the male has remained in its North American habitat. The water weed even blooms in some places in Europe but it cannot form seeds.

The Canadian water weed grows in shallow waters and roots in mud even at a depth of up to 10 m (33 ft), or floats freely. The weed grows so thickly on the water that it prevents the sun from warming it, suffocates other plants, restricts the movement of fish, and encourages the water to decompose.

Canadian water weed came to Europe suddenly, appearing in Ire-

A striking feature of the Water hyacinth **are the inflated leaf stalks. A detail of a leaf** *(right)*.

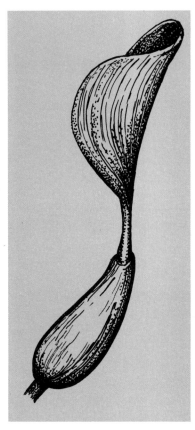

The Water hyacinth, **another plant capable of propagating with breath-taking speed.**

land and Scotland around 1840. We do not know what exactly happened, but believe that it was transported there by fish or on the backs of birds, or was planted by man. The genus name *Elodea* arose from the French pronunciation of the scientific name *Helodia*, which is derived from the Greek *helodes*, meaning marshy. It is difficult to believe that this unusual plant, growing in garden pools, can sometimes cause trouble to the breeders of fish and waterfowl, and even hamper boats.

The **Water hyacinth** (*Eichhornia crassipes*) not only propagates vigorously but, in contrast to the Canadian water weed, also has a lovely flower. The ornamental light mauve flowers grow in dense clusters from the tough leaves, shaped like shallow cornets, and an interestingly swollen stem. The air sacs on the stems are filled with a network of sparse fibres which hold the plant on the surface. It would be hard to find another plant with such apparent zest for life. It propagates so rapidly that within a short time it could cover the whole globe. The number of plants doubles in a fortnight, and within a year a single plant produces 17—20 million offspring. In this way it increases its volume 67 million times. This incomprehensible quantity could theoretically spread over the water surface of the whole world within two years!

Such calculations, however, did not enter the head of one of the admirers of the water hyacinth, a travelling businessman from Louisiana, U.S.A. He brought back this striking plant from a trip to Brazil, as did other researchers, missionaries and businessmen. He planted it in the quiet stream running near his home and went off again. When, after some time, he returned home he could not recognize his garden. The water hyacinth was growing everywhere. Just as the plant has spread through America, so it has also multiplied in Egypt and the Sudan, on the Nile and its tributaries. It is impossible to exterminate it mechanically in the sun-warmed tropical and sub-tropical waters, and effective chemicals would also poison the water.

Spreading Potatoes

The **Potato** (*Solanum tuberosum*) has undergone a long and interesting journey. There is a long history of the potato being grown as a crop. In the Peruvian Andes, where it originates, the Incas and other Indians grew potatoes several thousand years ago and used its image to decorate clay bowls. The potato is the greatest gift of the Peruvian countryside to world agriculture.

Insofar as we know, the Incas cultivated around 250 species of potatoes of various colours: from white and yellow, to pink, brown and black. It was the basic food of the Indians in the Andes — they ate them every day, whether fresh or dried. Since the small tubers contain up to 70 per cent water they are quite succulent. And

dried, they keep well as *chuňo*. To this day the Peruvians dry their potatoes in the traditional way — by sun during the day, and at night in the frost of the mountains. The remaining water in the partially dried tubers is stamped out under foot.

The potato tubers must be protected from direct light so that they do not turn green. In the parts

The edible potato tubers grow on the roots of the fruit-bearing plant.

of the plant subjected to light, a poison is formed. Potatoes usually contain 0.002—0.1 per cent of this chemical; old potatoes around 0.6 per cent, the shoots about 0.5 per cent, and the seeds as much as 1 per cent.

Around 0.3 per cent will make a poison, which can be obtained from approximately 0.5 kg (1 lb) of potatoes that have turned green. But in addition to water and starch, the young tubers of potatoes also contain a lot of valuable vitamin C, some group B vitamins, proteins, fibre, fat, potassium and amino-acids. For the Indians, the potato was a medicine as well as a food. They placed raw slices of potato on wounds and broken bones, and used them to cure internal infections.

Europeans discovered the potato in South America in the first half of the 16th century. The discovery is ascribed to a group of Spanish soldiers, commanded by Gonzales de Quesada, who first saw 'loury, tasty roots' in the Indian village of Sorokota in present day Colombia in 1536. They called them 'truffles', the name later spreading to Italy (*tartufo, tartufolo*). From this developed the German *kartoffel*, and the Russian *kartofel*. Another German word for the potato, *erdapfel* (earth apple), is derived from a translation of the French *pomme de terre*.

It is not known when and by whom the first potatoes were brought across the ocean to Europe. In fact, the first potatoes were not true potatoes but the edible rhizomes of the **Sweet potato** (*Ipomoea batatas*). But the name remained and *batata* turned into *patata* in Spanish, potato in English, and *potate* in Italian, as the name for the true potato.

After some confusion, the new plant was imported and grown as an ornamental garden plant at the end of the 16th century in Ireland,

The Sweet potato **with its edible rhizome** *(right).*

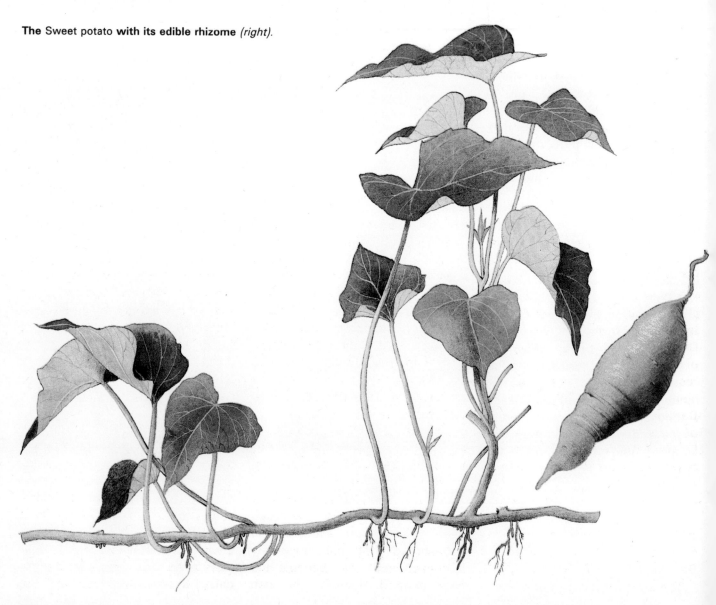

In the late 18th century potato flowers were presented in nosegays (small bunches of flowers), as a great rarity.

in Wrocław and Frankfurt. It was also grown in the imperial gardens of Maximillian II (1527—1576) by his court botanist Carolus Clusius.

It is recounted that King Philip II (1527—1598) received the first potatoes in 1565 from the Inca city of Cuzco in Peru. He sent some of them to the Pope to help him recover from a long illness. The novelty then found its way to the Cardinal in Flanders, to the Prefect of Mons, and finally to the court of Emperor Maximillian II, whose botanist Clusius was the first to write a description of the plant. He gave it the name of *Papas peruanorum*. The name used today, *Solanum tuberosum*, was taken over by Linné from the Basel physician Gaspard Bauhin (1560—1624).

The potato reached France, and also Germany and Italy, at the beginning of the 17th century. The French chemist Antoine Augustin Parmentier (1737—1813) was so enthusiastic about the potato that it made him famous. In 1780 he presented a bunch of potato flowers to King Louis XVI (1754—1793), who wore the flowers pinned to his coat as a nosegay. It was due to Parmentier that the potato was then grown, not only as an ornamental plant but for food. Since his death (1813) his grave has been adorned with the flowering potatoes.

Potatoes played an important role in Ireland too. They grew well, were good to eat, and were so widespread that their popularity increased until they became the national food. However, the Irish

relied so heavily on each new crop that a sudden failure caused by blight resulted in a national catastrophe, and many starved. In the middle of the last century, potatoes were the only food the poor could afford. One million died of malnutrition and the same number emigrated from the island to seek a better life in North America. Nevertheless, the Irish did not lose their faith in the potato because of the blight. They took healthy tubers with them to their new home. Thus the South American tuber found its way to North America, via the Irish.

Potatoes played an important role in European wars. It is said that they helped the people to survive difficult times of famine during the Thirty Year's War — though the serfs had no confidence in the 'poisonous' tubers, and could not accustom themselves to the new crop. For a long time they considered it to be a whim of aristocratic chefs. There were even local uprisings, the so-called potato wars. However, the

Traditional drying of Maize **cobs.**

As seen here, the cobs of different varieties of Maize **differ in colour, size and grain shape.**

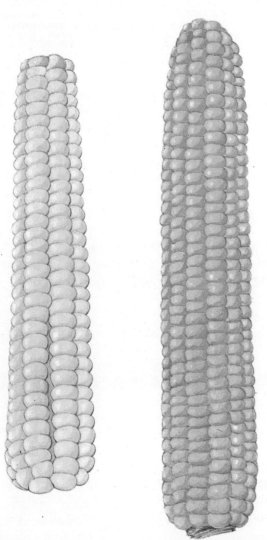

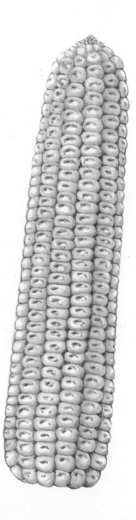

famine following the Seven Years' War did more to promote the cultivation of potatoes than the preaching of priests or orders from the Prussian King Frederick II (1712—1786).

This modest plant took such a foothold in Europe that it is now grown on many millions of acres of farmland, and we could hardly imagine a daily meal without it. From being an ornamental and then a fodder plant (in 18th century Germany and France), it soon appeared on all tables as an excellent and indispensable food.

Indian maize (*Zea mays*) is the sole American contribution to the world's list of key cereals. It has been cultivated for several thousand years, and during that time has substantially changed in appearance and use. We cannot be more explicit, because the wild ancestor has long disappeared and cannot be compared with the existing plant. However, we do know that maize was the main crop on the fields of American Indians from the coast up to an altitude of 3,500 m (11,490 ft). The most popular crop was a species of maize suitable for roasting. The Indians made a paste from the roasted cereal, from which they then made bread. The cereal was also the basis for producing an alcoholic drink called *chichu*, which the Americans later converted into whisky. Maize therefore plays a part in the production of Bourbon-whisky, alongside malt, which is made from barley and rye.

Maize was probably first cultivated by Mexican Indians. Since cultivating the cereal was such demanding work (in large part due to primitive methods and equipment), the village priests carried out religious rites, sang hymns and maintained long periods of fasting to ensure a good harvest. Indian women also tried to influence the harvest. The American poet H. W. Longfellow (1807—1882) describes, in his *Song of Hiawatha*, an Indian girl who undresses in the night and drags her robe around the maize field. This mystical rite was supposed to ensure a better crop. Further, meticulous methods were described by P. A. Mattioli (1500—1577) in his *Botanical Herbarium* in the 16th century: 'The Indians plant maize as follows: several of them go to the fields together and stand in a regular row, one beside another. With a pointed stick in the right hand they make a hole in the ground into which they place four to five grains, pressing them in with their right foot so that the parrots do not scratch them out and peck at them. They then take three steps forward, again plant seeds, and so continue until the whole field is set. Before planting, they always soak the seeds for two days and do not plant before the soil has been moistened by rain. The grains germinate very quickly.'

There are many myths and legends revealing the strong links between maize and Indian life. The ancient Mayas and the Aztecs revered maize as a gift from the gods, believing that man was not made of clay but of maize grains ground to flour. We find a term for maize in all ancient Indian languages. Furthermore, maize grains were found in the tombs of Indians as food for the long journey after death.

The first grain was brought to Europe by the navigator Christopher Columbus (1451—1506) in 1493. He thus assisted one of the most important cereals on its grand excursion into the world. Initially it took small steps through Europe as a garden rarity and then, more rapidly than the potato, spread through the Old World and Asia. As a warmth-loving plant, it soon found a home not only in Spain but throughout the Mediterranean region, particularly in France and Italy, and also in the

Near East and in Turkey from where it journeyed with man across the Balkans to central Europe as 'Turkish wheat' in the first half of the 17th century. The Portuguese took it to Africa, India, China, and Java.

Even today, maize continues to maintain its position as the cereal with the biggest yield in the world. And it is put to many different uses. Dishes made from maize include the Italian polenta, Rumanian mamaliga, Mexican tortillas, North American hominy, and the Swiss Türkenriebel. Maize is also boiled as corn on the cob, and used for cornflakes and puffed corn.

Drinks including syrup, wine, liqueurs, spirits and beer, are also made from maize. The cobs, the whole plants, or just the straw, are fed to cattle or used as animal bedding. Both edible and industrial oils are pressed from the grain for lighting, for oiling machinery, for making soap and for use in paints. The axis of the cob can be made into replacements for corks. The fibre from the stems is a raw material for the production of celluloid, paper, insulation coverings, for stuffing in upholstery and for the production of linoleum. The dried bracts protecting the cobs are made into many items, including woven mats, bags and hats. A drug derived from the dried styles and stigmas of the female flowers places the plant among medicinal herbs. The delicate silks are a popular diuretic and slimming cure in folk medicine.

While maize is quite dependent on the care and assistance of man, **Horseradish** (*Armoracia rusticana*) is a crop that is very independent. Not only does it grow without our assistance, flowering and propagating, it also spreads itself — over short and quite long distances. Horseradish originated in eastern Europe and the neighbouring parts of west Asia. Then it

The Horseradish **flower** *(left)* **and its root** *(right)*, **which can quickly produce new plants.**

found a new habitat in central and east Asia, North and South America, in New Zealand and throughout the whole of Europe. It grows on soils rich in nutrients, close to human settlements, as well as on the banks of ponds and waterways, and in ditches.

The cultivation of horseradish as a garden plant is mentioned in the 12th century by the educated German abbess, Hildëgard of Bingen (1098—1179). Even then, horseradish was used in the kitchen as a flavouring and as a stimulating relish with meat. In measured doses it has a curative effect, aid-

The moisture-loving Sweet flag.

applied to relieve rheumatism. The poultices are made from freshly grated horseradish which has a sharp smell. It contains the essential oil of mustard, twice as much vitamin C as lemon, and also fytoncides — herbal exterminators which restrict the propagation of bacteria, moulds and viruses. Finally, this useful plant has an astonishing ability to propagate. Every piece of root has a large number of buds which are easily brought to life, growing into new plants.

A Disappointing Rarity

The slender plant **Sweet flag** (*Acorus calamus*) grows around lakes and pools, among sedges, reeds and rushes, and on marshy banks. Europeans have only known this plant since the second half of the 16th century. Up until then it was known and enjoyed only as the candied rhizomes which German chemists used to import directly from Constantinople, and sold as a precious sweet from Turkey. The first plants on European soil were grown as a rarity in 1574 by the botanist Clusius in the Viennese Botanical Gardens. He was presented with a live root by a diplomat from Constantinople, and planted it with ceremony on the banks of a pool in one of the first botanical gardens in the world. The rhizome took root and formed several spear-like leaves, flowering after three years.

A green cluster of small yellow-green flowers grows at an angle from the flat, three-sided stems, as if bent from a leaf. However, the pointed leaf above the flower is, in fact, an arum-like sheath, similar to the white sheath of the marsh marigold. The inconspicuous little flowers turn into red berries in their original homeland, but in the northern hemisphere the fruit does not ripen. The sweet flag

has proved a disappointment as a decorative, exotic plant, and its appearance has fallen short of expectations. It has been likened to a reed and received the Latin name *Acorus calamus,* meaning ill-favoured reed.

Weeds Among the Cultures

Plants which are intentionally grown in fields, gardens and vineyards are called cultivated plants and their growth cultures. All other plants which are not supposed to be there, which grow unwanted, are called weeds. They are not a unified group. Weeds include annuals and perennials, small and large plants, plants with attractive and ornamental flowers, those with inconspicuous flowers, creeping plants, medical herbs, poisonous plants, and many others.

The definition of a weed depends on what you are trying to grow, and in which part of the world. For example, if domestic plants spread to agricultural land, they become a nuisance and can be termed weeds. So, for instance, in Afghanistan there is a wild melon that has infiltrated fields of sorghum, maize and cotton. What in an English garden would be highly prized, in this context is a nuisance — a weed to be got rid of. There is

Weeds can be annual or perennial, minute or creeping, flowering inconspicuously or with delightful, ornamental flowers. All propagate readily, whether by seed or root section. Illustrated here are several brightly-flowering field weeds: **(1)** Corn poppy — **poppyhead and seed (2)** Field poppy — **poppyhead (3)** Cornflower — **a section of the flower cluster and seed box (4)** Discoid chamomile — **a cross-section of flower head and pod (5)** Shepherd's purse; *left,* **a plant attacked by the mould** *Albugo candida; far left,* **the fruit and its cross-section (6)** Wild radish — **fruit and seed (7)** Charlock, **or** Wild mustard, **with its seed on the** *right.*

ing digestion and getting rid of spring weariness. In addition horseradish poultices are briefly

another example of an exotic weed, which grows in the Mongolian fields. It has the poetic name of Golden thread. Its medicinal properties were described by the scholar Avicenna (980—1037) and it was used for hundreds of years as a laxative and to stop bleeding.

Field poppy (*Papaver rhoeas*) originates from south-east Europe. Today, however, it is a spreading field weed found amongst cereals, root crops, legumes, rape, and other European crops, and in Asia, north Africa, North America, Australia and New Zealand. It grows mainly on heavy soils in warmer regions. However, after many years the farmers are gradually winning the battle and are shifting it from the fields to their edges, to wasteland, road verges, rubbish tips and fallow land.

The simple beauty of the bright red flower is at first enclosed in the bud in the projecting hairy calyx. When the flower blooms it straightens itself, both sepals of the calyx drop off and free the four petals with a thick, smooth stigma in the centre, surrounded by thin black filaments. The ripe capsule, the poppy-head, contains several hundred seeds, more than enough to ensure another generation. The poppy-head has several openings under the lobed stigma so that, when the wind blows, its seeds are scattered evenly around the plant.

The **Cornflower** (*Centaurea cyanus*) has been spreading round the world via fields of cereals since the Neolithic era about 8,000 years ago. Its original habitat was the Near East and the eastern Mediterranean. However, we now find it wherever wheat is grown. Along with the red flowers of the field poppy and the purple corn cockle, the cornflower helped until recently to brighten the uniform colour of fields of ripening wheat. But it also meant anxious times for the farmer because several hun-

dred seed capsules ripen on a single plant, all capable of germinating over a two- or three- year period. The seeds are scattered over the field together with improperly cleaned grain. With more efficient cleaning, the numbers of annual cornflower have considerably lessened. Nonetheless, it can still be found where fields are farmed in the old way. Indeed, it should not disappear entirely because we should not only be losing an unwanted weed but also one of the medicinal herbs of both folk and orthodox medicine. The bright blue flower heads of the cornflower are a diuretic. In France, a tincture made from the plant is used in eye treatment.

Pliny the Elder reported the healing power of the cornflower in the 1st century A.D. He said that the centaur Chiron used cornflower to heal the wound on his leg inflicted by Hercules' arrow. Another interpretation of the name relates to the value of the cornflower as a medicinal herb, and translates its name as *centum*, meaning 100, and *aurum*, meaning gold.

A cross-section of **Pineapple weed** or **Discoid chamomile** (*Matricaria matricarioides*) reveals a hollow, cone-shaped receptacle as found in its relative the wild chamomile (*Matricaria chamomilla*). However, it lacks the white florets. The whole plant is strongly aromatic because it contains a quantity of essential oil. Yet it does not contain various chemicals which can be used in medicines, and so cannot be substituted for the true chamomile.

While wild chamomile has been grown amongst field crops since pre-historic times, there are various parts of the world where it is relatively new. Having originated in North America and northern Asia, it was carried to South America and Europe, and now grows as far as the arctic and antarctic.

To begin with, as is the case with many plants, chamomile was first grown in Europe in botanical gardens, as a specimen of North American vegetation. Its occurrence in the wild was first noted by botanists near Berlin in 1852, one year later near Prague, and in 1889 near Vienna. From the beginning of the 20th century it has spread rapidly.

In fields of winter wheat it is a harmless weed. However, its strong scent persistently spoils crops for animal feed. We most frequently find discoid chamomile on the edges of fields, and in places where people frequently walk. However, it does not mind being stepped on. On the contrary, this is one way in which its seeds can be spread. The bottom of shoes can be excellent carriers, transporting capsules containing thousands of light seeds. In just one year, a single plant produces up to 5,000 fruits. In damp weather the capsules become slimy, and this helps them to stick to the feet of people and animals, and even to car tyres. What is more, discoid chamomile is unaffected by drought and cold, and will grow in most kinds of soil.

Several thousand seeds also ripen on the **Shepherd's purse** (*Capsella bursa pastoris*). Its tiny white flowers, born in clusters, are very short-lived. The plant also has strikingly shaped fruits, resembling a small purse, or shepherd's purse, which has given the plant its name.

Shepherd's purse is an annual plant, and it makes the utmost use of that one year. It begins to grow at the end of winter, and eventually produces an abundance of flow-

Map showing the world-wide cultivation ▶ of Rye (1) An ear of rye (2) Types of wheat ears (3) A barley ear (4) An oat ear.

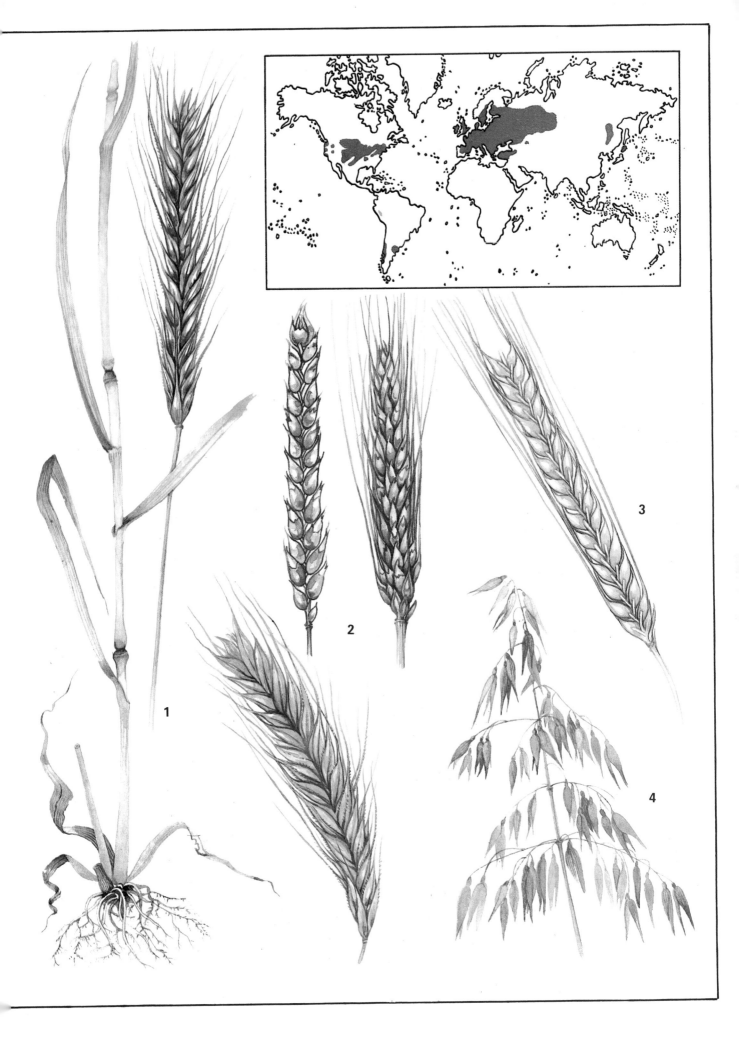

1

2

3

4

ers that continue to appear until the start of the next winter. It is such an inconspicuous plant that it is not surprising it has spread from its original habitat, in the Mediterranean, with cereals into cultivated and fallow land, perhaps all over the world. It has even spread up the slopes of the Alps to a height of 3,800 m (12,470 ft) above sea level.

We can often find among other plants some that have whitish, twisted stems. This is a disease caused by a parasitic fungus, white mould (*Albugo candida*). Such plants contaminate the shepherd's purse, preventing a drug being made from it when dried out, which stops internal bleeding. In eastern Asia we find shepherd's purse used in the kitchen. In Korea, the young leaves, with their high protein content, are used as a vegetable in soups, or are added to a special vegetable mixture called *kimchi*.

Another plant which grows amongst cereal crops is the south European weed **Wild radish** (*Raphanus raphanistrum*). It spreads through the world along with cultivated cereals. Wherever cereals grow there is their faithful companion the wild radish, a member of the Brassica family (*Brassicaceae*). It has light yellow flowers with delicate mauve veins, which make it easy to identify. The **Charlock** or **Wild mustard** (*Sinapis arvensis*) looks similar, but has sepals that stand out. The fruit of both plants are also similar, but differ in one way. The radish has a pod that splits across into sections with the seeds enclosed. The charlock has a side lid that opens — the seeds are inside, fastened to the rim.

Once a Weed, Later a Cereal

The life story of **Rye** (*Secale cereale*) is most unusual. Some plants which are now useful used to be sought by man in the wild, and were cultivated in gardens. It was quite different with rye. This plant asserted itself without help. The wild grass *Secale segetale*, a native of the near East and the Caucasus, was one of the weeds that spread through Europe via wheat and barley fields. It is a tall grass whose small grains made it the only wild kind of rye to have ears that did not disintegrate. It bears up well under the harsh climatic conditions of the north and at heights of up to 2,000 m (6,565 ft), making it a fairly easily grown and a popular cereal. There is now a new cereal which is a cross between rye and wheat. It is called *Triticale*, and has wheat-like grains and grows under even more difficult conditions.

Rye was not known in ancient Babylon and Egypt. However, it was known in Greece and Rome, though it was not highly regarded. We learn from *Naturalis Historia*, written by Pliny the Elder in the first century A.D., that the grains were too small and the bread black. The dark flour was improved by the addition of wheat flour.

Rye was first grown in the Bronze Age, 2,500—900 years B.C. in Europe. It was later grown by the Slavs, who in turn passed it on to the Germans. Today, however, rye is not widely grown in west Europe, or in North America, where people prefer **Oats** (*Avena sativa*). It is believed that oats were originally weeds that appeared in fields of rye, and which were later collected and grown by themselves.

The oat was certainly a weed in Greek and Roman times. Some attention was paid to oats by the ancient Greek physician Dieuches, in the 4th century B.C., and he promoted porridge made from oats as an easily digestible food.

Oats are generally chosen as an easy-to-grow cereal for higher altitudes, and especially as food for horses, giving their coats a healthy shine. Oats are also grown because they can be used for medicinal and cosmetic purposes. They provide strength, help people who cannot sleep or eat, and also reduce blood pressure. Porridge, made from oats, is a popular and healthy meal, being rich in vitamin B. In addition, oatmeal used in the bath is a good remedy for sensitive skins.

Map showing the cultivation of Oat. Also (1) The flowering oat and (5) Its grain — on the *left* is its true size, on the *right* two images differently enlarged. The hairy, spindle-like grains of oats are enclosed in a husk and the hull, and differ from the grains of other cereals (2) Grains of wheat are egg-shaped with a deep groove; the husks of the grain are usually without slender bristles (an awn), though sometimes they do end with them. In the *centre* — true size; *around* — enlarged grains shown from various sides (3) The elongated grains of rye after they have dropped out of the loose husks: true size on the *left,* enlarged grain viewed from the side on the *right* (4) Barley grains: *centre* — true size; *around* and *below* enlarged side view. The long-awned husks and the hull grow firmly attached to the ripe grain (6) Maize grains are smooth and shiny or wrinkled on the outside. *Left* of the enlarged grain are a number of views of the grain, true size (7) The round grain of millet is enclosed in the shiny case of the husk and hull. It is coloured light and deep beige, red-beige, and brown to purple, according to variety. On the *left*, the grain, true size. On the *right*, a much-enlarged grain.

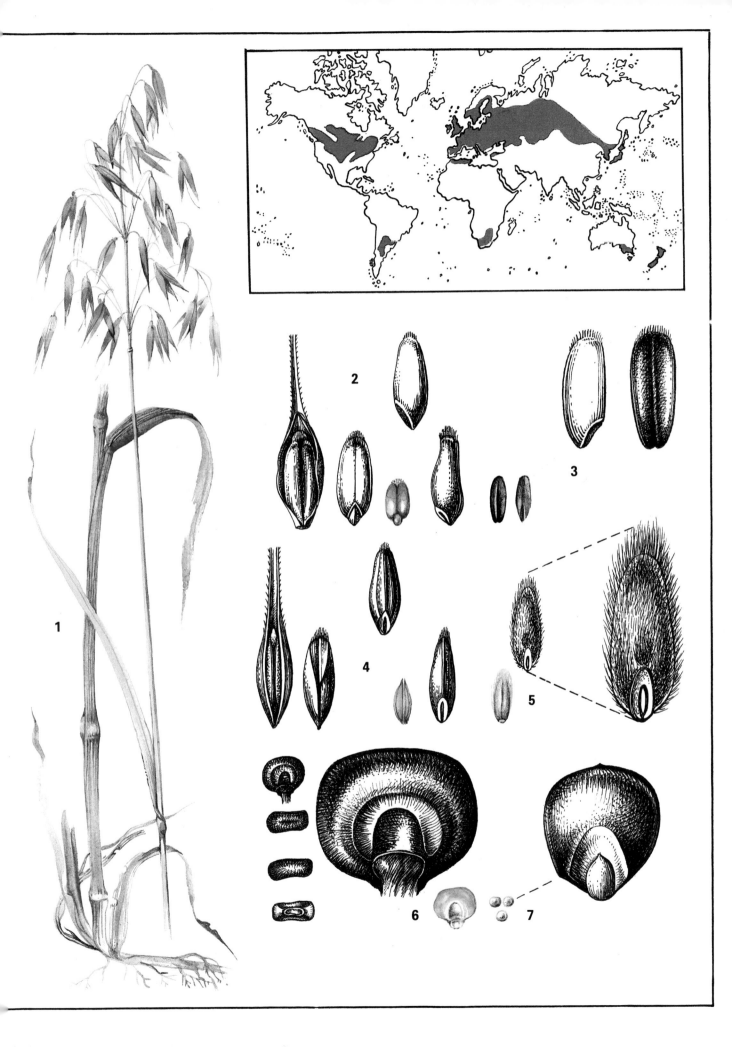

An Excellent Companion

It is true that 'Man cannot live by bread alone'. People also need beautiful things to look at, such as flowers. And so, from the dawn of history, mankind has grown not just plants for food and medicine, but to brighten his surroundings. Of all the attractive flowers, the **Rose** (*Rosa*) is for many people the most exciting. It has been cultivated for more than 5,000 years, having first appeared as a wild rose in the near East.

Earliest mention of the rose was found during excavations of the towns of Ur and Akkad from the time of King Sargon, 2,600 years B.C. The picture of a rose in the paintings at Knossos on Crete date from 2,000 B.C., and in Babylonian paintings from 540 B.C. Confucius (551—479 B.C.) writes about roses in the imperial garden in Peking in 500 B.C., and in 428 B.C. Herodes described the rose of King Hidas which had 60 petals. Theophrastus makes first mention in 287 B.C. of the **Dogrose** (*Rosa canina*), and of a rose of 100 petals. The Greeks looked upon the rose, like the lily, as a symbol of beauty, love and youth. It was very popular with the Romans and Egyptians, as well, and to this day is highly prized.

The rose reached Europe during the Turkish crusades. The famous rose gardens of France are first mentioned in the 6th century A.D. Later, the assortment of roses grown at the turn of the 18th and 19th centuries was further increased by a better transport system. Chinese, Japanese and Indian roses were now sent abroad.

Some species of roses are not only delightful to look at. For example, the **Damascene rose** (*Rosa damascena*), the **White rose** (*Rosa alba*), and the **100-petal rose** (*Rosa centifolia*) are grown for their fragrant oils. The petals are gathered by hand. About 3,000 to 4,000 kg (1,360—1,815 lb) of petals are gathered from 2.5 acres (1 hectare) from which about 1 kg (35 oz) of the oil is produced. It is mainly used in cosmetics and perfumes, but also in confectionery. The ancient Greeks and Romans made perfumes from rose petals, and medicines from rose hips (the berries that appear in the autumn).

The Steppe Runner

From a distance, the flowering **Tartar kale** (*Crambe tataria*) looks like a flock of sheep scattered in spring over the green grass. The quantity of tiny four-petalled flowers shows that tartar kale belongs to the *Brassicaceae* family. Because of the unusual manner of distributing its seeds, it is sometimes called the 'steppe runner'. It demonstrates this skill in the autumn, when its large quantity of fruit, the pear-shaped pods, ripen, and the branching part of the plant

A formal arrangement of roses.

The ornamental rose bush has been cultivated for over 5,000 years, longer than any of its rivals. There is even a mention of famous rose gardens in France at the beginning of the 6th century. Here we see the blooms of cultivated roses: (1) The 100-petal rose (2) The Damascene rose (3) The Hybrid tea rose (4) The Crumpled dog rose.

The flowering Tartar kale.

above ground dries. The winter wind, which blows hard across the bare slopes of the Russian steppes (or plains), snatches up the bushy part of the plant and rolls it away. Tartar kale drops its seeds as it rolls, and wherever they drop, a new plant grows in the spring.

Tartar kale is a plant of the east European and Siberian steppes. There is another kind of kale growing on the sea coast of western and northern Europe. The salt loving **Sea-kale** (*Crambe maritima*) is grown in some places as a vegetable, the white fleshy shoots resembling asparagus.

V ENGINEERING ROOTS

The selected plants in this section are but a few examples of the ways in which nature has influenced the way we live, and the look of our cities. Some of our greatest engineering and technical achievements result from scientists copying the natural world.

The Aerial Route

By the time the fresh green carpet of spring grass is brightened with the golden suns of the **Dandelion** (*Taraxacum officinale*), the ground has already warmed up. The golden flower heads smell of honey.

The Dandelion's 'parachute' inspired Leonardo da Vinci to design a man-carrying parachute. As shown here, the idea clearly worked. ▼

The ripe fruit seeds of the Dandelion are ▶ carried off by the wind, until the head is left bare.

The hard-working bees find in them a quantity of pollen, and they also pollinate these plants.

Travelling by air is no problem for the dandelion seeds. The ripening fruits are attached to a long parachute of white hairs. They rest on top of the flower stalk, waiting for a breath of wind. When the breeze catches the balls of fine hairs it lifts them away and carries them over the countryside. They drop slowly to earth like parachutists. This is probably what inspired Leonardo da Vinci (1452—1519) at the end of the 15th century, to invent and design a parachute. However, this is only one of many examples of plants sending out their flying seeds on an aerial journey.

The sturdy tree, the **Common ash** (*Fraxinus excelsior*) also entrusts its seeds, enclosed in cap-

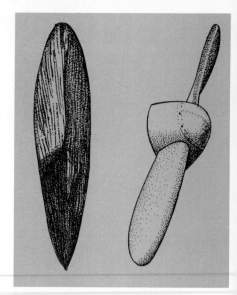

The Common ash — **the flowering and fruit-bearing twigs.**

A clear example of the similarity between the shape of an aeroplane propeller and the seed of the Common ash.

sules, to air transport. We find the ash has similar winged 'keys' to the maple, but they are of a slightly different shape. The long, oval-shaped, gently curved wings form propellers similar to those of a plane. And the capsule 'flies' in a very similar manner to a plane.

The round fruits of the **Zanonia**

A propeller with three blades.

(*Zanonia macrocarpa*) are hard and leathery. They hang loosely in the crown of the trees, up which the green vine climbs to reach towards the tropical sun. The fruits, 20—24 cm (8—9 in) in diameter, swing lightly in the breeze until one or other of them splits and opens up to form a bell shape. The seeds, set in dense rows, can now escape. Each winged seed is very light (one third of a gramme), and is carried on silkily shining and flexible wings which are 14 to 16 cm (5—6 in) across. This is altogether the largest wing span of any seed. The wings make it possible for a perfect, slow, gliding flight in large spirals under almost windless conditions, and have influenced aircraft wing design.

The ancient story of Icarus describes man' first attempt to imitate bird flight by fastening on wings. This was a flight driven by arm movement. However, in the case of winged seeds there is no effort. All that is needed is wind. Yet if the wind can carry a seed, could it not also carry man? That is what the pioneers of flight thought and at the end of the last century they started to try out their ideas. Mostly, they tried them out on themselves and on machines of their own construction.

The German aviator Otto Lilienthal (1848—1896) achieved a gliding flight over several hundred metres. After his tragic death the Austrian aviator, Igo Etrich (1879—1967), carried on with his work. For a very long time he took his cue from nature, observing how birds and bats flew, in his attempts to construct flying machines. Yet he never succeeded because of the problems in constructing flexible wings.

By accident, he found a better model to copy. He read an article, written by a teacher from Hamburg, describing the perfect flying ability of the fruits of the Sunda Island Zanonia vine. He obtained

A hang glider, originally based on the 'flying' fruits of the Zanonia.

a sample of the seed from the author, and this discovery launched the early years (which lasted from 1904—1909) of gliders of the 'flying wing' type, without a tail tiller. The first two models had a wing span of 6 and 10 m (19.5 and 32 ft), could carry a weight of 25 and 70 kg (55—154 lb) but could not carry a person. It was not until 1907 that

The flying fruit of the Zanonia *(top)* and a man-made wing *(below)*.

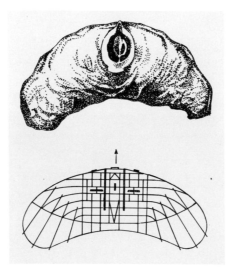

Igo Etrich constructed a glider named **Taube** (Dove), which he successfully demonstrated in Vienna in 1909.

Another example of nature showing man how to fly concerns the **Red maple** (*Acer platanoides*), with its fruits and winged capsules. The wings are sited on either side of the capsule, inside which are the seeds. A light breeze disturbs the branches, and the capsules are carried off in all directions. Thanks to the wings, the fruits do not fall straight down, where the seedlings would not grow well in the shade of the bushy, spreading crown of the tree, but land further away where there is space to grow. Provided there are no unfavourable circular wind movements, a light wind can carry the winged capsules over a distance of up to 100 m (328 ft). Should the seeds catch a rising stream of air they are carried much farther.

The flight of the winged capsules is influenced by their design. When the wind drops, the cap-

The design of the helicopter, and a windmill's sail, came from the capsules of the Red maple.

sules flutter straight to the ground, rather like a helicopter making a vertical descent.

The Value of Examples

The Mangrove (*Rhizophora*) is the commonest tree growing on the coast of tropical seas. Dense bands of impenetrable growth, often several kilometres wide, border the tide-free coast around the equator, and often extend beyond both tropics. In the soft, permanently boggy soil, the trees are anchored not by one root, but a number of arched roots growing from the trunk and lower branches. It is as if you spread out your fingers on top of a table, and raise your arm straight up above them. The fingers represent the tree's roots, your arm the trunk of the tree. The mass of roots keeps the tree beyond the reach of the moving sea.

The people who live in this area build their houses in a similar way. They support them on stilts, which keep the rooms high above the water.

The mangrove forest grows rapidly thanks to its unusual way of producing new young trees. The seeds do not leave the 'mother' tree until they have begun to grow into miniature trees, complete with open leaves. Thousands of young plants hang from the branches of the 'maternal' trees until they are over 0.5 m (1.6 ft) in length. Then they drop under their own weight, with most of them taking root at once, right below the main tree, where they form a dense undergrowth. Should a seedling be carried away by a stream of water to another suitable, undisturbed spot, it will not be long before another forest of salt-loving trees springs up, growing up to 50 m (18 ft) high.

Left: Red maple **(seeded fruit and leaf).** *Right:* Sycamore maple **(seeded fruit and leaf).**

A helicopter lands by auto-rotation.

The Mangrove — a tree with stilt-like roots.

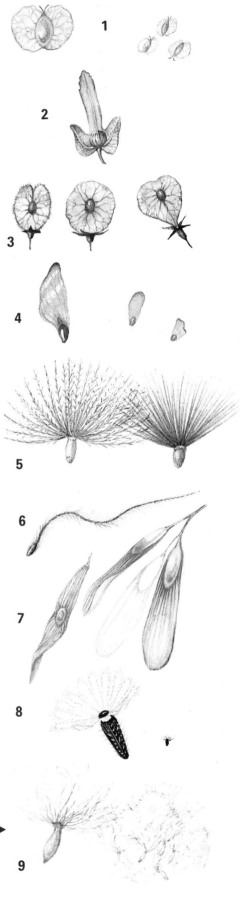

There is no need to say too much about the similarity of bell flower shapes, to church bells. It is evident at first glance. The family name of the plant has a Latin origin, coming from the word *campana*, meaning bell. But that was not given until the 16th century when the German botanist and physician, Leonard Fuchs (1501—1566), first used the name *Campanula* for bells.

The funnel-shaped, purplish-blue corolla of the **Rover bellflower** (*Campanula rapunculoides*) is divided into five 'petals' to almost half its depth. Pushing up from its centre is the stigma, looking like the tongue of the bell.

Incidentally the metal used to make a bell is a bronze mixture of copper and tin. In order for the bell to be able to swing, it is loosely hung from a loop at its top, fixed to a beam in the bell tower. When

Examples of some flying fruits and seeds: **(1)** Birch **(enlarged fruit on the** *left*) **(2)** Hornbeam **(3)** *Ailanthus karpinifolia, Ailanthus glandulosa, Fraxinus arnus* **(4)** Pine, spruce, fir **(5)** Teasel **and** thistle **(6)** Anemone **(7)** *Ailanthus glandulosa* **and** *Fraxinus arnus* **(8)** Gallant soldier **(9)** Poplar **(enlarged fruit on the** *left*).

Stilts lift the homes of the natives to safe heights.

the bell is set in motion, the clapper strikes its sides. This musical percussion instrument, which has for centuries rung out from the belfries of churches, is said to be giving a false tone in recent years. This is caused by the acid rain which is corroding the bell metal.

The Hygrometer and the Compass

A hygrometer is an apparatus for measuring humidity — that is, the amount of moisture in the atmosphere. A simple hygrometer is very easy to make. You need a small box, a pin and, most important, the ripe fruit of the **Common stork's**

bill (*Erodium cicutarium*). The plant lies close to the ground, where its glandulous, hairy stems with feathery leaves are spread out in circular clumps. The pinkish flowers and beak-shaped fruits betray the plant's relationship to the geranium family (*Geraniaceae*).

The fruit has an immensely long beak, enclosing five smooth seeds. When ripe, the capsule divides up into five separate lobes, each containing one seed. Each lobe is equipped with a long, spiral-shaped spike which is sensitive to humidity. The spike straightens out in damp weather, and curls up when dry. The changes between damp and dry weather force the spike to

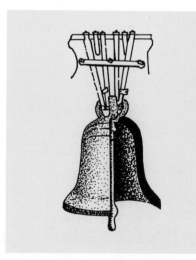

Cross-section of a bell in a belfry.

Rover bellflower.

a scale revealing how much dampness is in the atmosphere.

The common stork's bill is an annual or a biennial plant. It grows in Europe on waste ground, and in dry grassy places.

Prickly lettuce (*Lactuca serriola*) is found in both Europe and America. It grows on sunny, rocky slopes, on hilly ground, on field boundaries and pathways, as well as on uncultivated ground and

Common stork's bill **with fruit** *(right)*.

move to and fro, so drilling the seed into the ground. The sensitivity of the spike to humidity and its resultant movement is similar to the mechanism on a hygroscope, which moves an indicator across

87

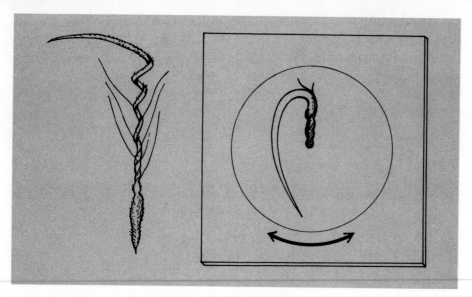

The spike of the separated seeds of the Common stork's bill is sensitive to humidity. It curls up when dry and straightens out when damp. The alternating movements drill the seed into the soil, where it rests until it germinates. We can use the sensitive spike as an indicator on a simple hygrometer *(right)* which can forecast the weather.

in related groundsel or dandelion — has been replaced by stiff spikes.

The scientific name of the plant is a translation of the Latin *bidens*, meaning two-toothed. This refers to the capsules which not only have two to four sharp spikes, but their edges and spikes which are covered with thorns. This is a simple but most effective clinging mechanism which easily grips anything with which the ripe plant comes into contact, whether it be the fur of an animal, the feathers of a bird, or the clothing of a person. And a seed capsule that falls into water can become attached to the mouth or gills of fish, preventing them from breathing and taking in food.

This accidental hooking of the seed, however, is similar to the intentional catching of fish on a hook, with a backward pointing barb to prevent the fish from es-

wasteland. Being exposed all day long to the sun enables it to make full use of its remarkable talent.

At midday, in full sunshine, the delicate leaves avoid the sun's fierce heat by turning over, so that only their edges are exposed to the sun high above them. However, in early morning and late afternoon the leaves face east and west, looking directly at the sun when it is not so powerful. In this way prickly lettuce is a natural compass, with the tips of the leaves pointing north-south, like the magnetic needle of a compass.

A Harpoon and an Anchor

Bur marigolds (*Bidens tripartita*) are annual plants with fruits that are well equipped to travel. The usual soft down of the seeds — as

The leaves of the Prickly lettuce are ► a natural compass indicating north-south.

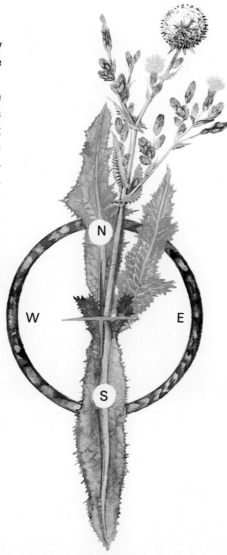

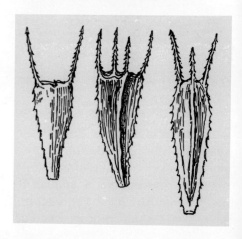

Propagation of the Bur marigold depends on the successful dispersion of the fruit and its seeds. The plant bears seed capsules whose toothed spikes resemble harpoons. It grows in marshy and damp places, in ditches, on the banks of streams, in water meadows, and in coastal thickets. Here are the capsules of several species of Bur marigold: *Bidens radiatus (left)*, *Bidens nutans*, *Bidens tripartita (right)*.

caping. The same principle is used for catching large sea fish. Although they are not caught with a rod, but with a harpoon thrown from fishing boats or shot from a gun, it has a pointed end with a barb, resembling the shape of the spike on the bur marigold seed.

Tripartite bur marigold (*Bidens tripartita*), like **Nodding bur marigold** (*Bidens nutans*), grows on marshy and boggy land where there is standing water. They are found almost across the whole of Europe, and north and west Asia. Nodding bur marigold grows in North America as well, while tripartite bur marigold has got as far as Australia.

On the quiet waters of ponds, pools and backwaters we sometimes find clusters of smallish, birch-like leaves. However, their stalks are puffed up in order to keep the heavy, ripening fruits from falling into the muddy water. The stalks of the leaves have a thin filling of airy fibres and act as floats.

The **Water chestnut** (*Trapa natans*) flowers from June to August with inconspicuous white flowers. Later the flowers turn into hard fruits, or nuts, which have a spiky exterior. They then drop downwards, like anchors, into the mud, where they spend the winter. In the spring a young plant grows from the seed, held to the bottom by the spikes. As it begins to develop so it releases itself coming up to the surface in late spring.

The soft centre of the water chestnut is nutritious and tasty. It contains proteins, fat and starch, from which a special flour is made. The water chestnut is therefore cultivated in plantations, especially in India, Japan and China.

A Splendid Invention

Sedges, which are part of a large family, grow in many species in the warm and damp regions of the tropics and subtropics. The sedge **Papyrus** (*Cyperus alternifolius*) is grown in greenhouses and as a house plant.

A similar plant, but one which grows an extraordinary 4—6 m (13—20 ft) high, and which has a wealth of tufts of leaves, is the **Egyptian paper reed** (*Cyperus papyrus*). Its history reaches back to ancient Egypt, over 6,000 years ago. At this time there were dense growths of papyrus on the marshy banks of the River Nile. They provided not only edible roots and raw material for ship building, making baskets, mats and ropes, but also, after the invention of a written alphabet, material for the production of the well-known papyrus. They were rolls of 'paper', very fine and thin (around 0.1 cm), flexible and white. The writer had to hold down the writhing roll with both hands before he could inscribe on it the hieroglyphs from left to right, and sometimes in vertical columns. He wrote with a small brush which he dipped into black or red dye, according to the importance of the text. When he made a mistake, he wiped it away with a damp rag, or licked it off! If a mistake was not discovered until later, when the ink had dried, the piece of paper had to be cut out and replaced with a clean piece of papyrus. Experts believe that since there was a high demand for the limited supplies of papyrus, people often washed their 'paper' clean when they had finished writing on it. This enabled them to use it over and over again.

A scientific explanation of the plant's name — *papyrus* — leads us to the original Egyptian term *pa-puro*, which means that which belongs to the king or Pharaoh. And indeed, production of papyrus was in the hands of the ruler himself.

A painting dating from 4,000 B.C. has been preserved, which shows the harvesting of papyrus stalks. However, Pliny the Elder gave a detailed written account of the production of papyrus rolls (the first person to do so). He described how thinly cut, long strips

The fruit of the Water chestnut, **in shape and function, recall a ship's anchor.**

The great Egyptian ruler Ti passes through a papyrus thicket.

An Egyptian papyrus scroll.

Morus. It is similar to the mulberry, also having large, lobed leaves covered with woolly hairs. It too is planted in the parks of southern Europe as an ornamental, shady tree. In its homeland of eastern Asia, it is one of the oldest plants put to practical use. Paper as delicate as silk but strong was produced from the approximately 2 cm (0.75 in) long fibres, obtained from the thick layers of the inner bark as far back as 105 A.D. It is called *kojo* in Japan.

The bark is peeled off the branches, which are submerged under water, and are then left to soak until the inner layer, the 'bast', separates. The bast is then mashed on a board into small fibres. This is then placed on

of the soft centre of the stalks were first placed alongside each other so that their edges overlapped. Other strips were then placed crosswise, creating another layer. Then another one was stuck on top. We do not know what sort of glue the ancient Egyptians used. When modern scientists attempted to copy the original production, the resultant paper was of inferior quality. It was brittle, easily broke, and it darkened as the glue seeped through to the surface.

The raw material for the fine Chinese and Japanese papers is provided by the eastern Asian tree **Paper mulberry** (*Broussonetia papyrifera*), which is related to the

A flowering branch of the Paper mulberry.

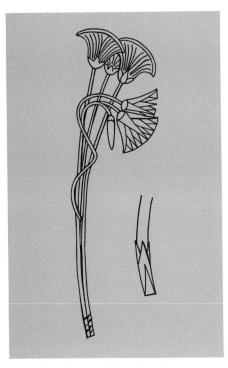

A stylized image of the Egyptian paper reed.

The bur of Great Burdock with hooked bristles *(left)* and Cocklebur *(far right).*

a strainer which is shaken, and the substance which falls through is rolled into paper, and then pressed out and dried. Paper made from the paper mulberry tree resembles paper made from cloth. It is like a very fine woven fabric, and is therefore also used to make handkerchiefs and as a light material for clothing.

Another, special kind of paper was made for ornamental printing. One example is the Chinese 'rice paper', made from thin leaves of the pith of the Chinese tree *Tetrapanax papyrifer.* Fibres from the stalks of sunflowers have also been used by the Chinese as a raw material for the production of paper.

A Simple Principle

The original of the practical and ever popular Velcro fastener is found in the bristling heads of the **Burdock** (*Arctium*) and **Cocklebur** (*Xanthium*). The outer sections which conceal the globular flower head, change into stiff tipped hooks, pointing inwards. After flowering, they cover the brownish seed pods. They germinate well, often a long way from the mother plant, because the little 'balls' or 'buttons' catch easily and hold fast to the fur of animals or the clothing of passing people.

They hold very firmly, as do the small, plastic hooks on a strip of material which are lightly pressed to another strip of hairy felt. Opening them is as quick and easy. These hook and loop fasteners (Velcro) are used on sportswear and shoes, and also for fastening bags and handbags.

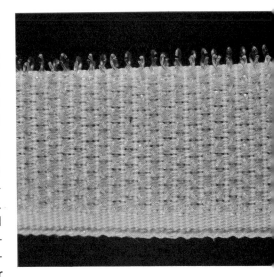

An enlarged Velcro hook.

A Shot at the End of Summer

Do you enjoy surprises? Try the reaction of Touch-me-not (*Impatiens nolitangere*). When ripe, the narrow pods are stretched to breaking point and the slightest touch or shock causes them to explode. The seams of the pods cannot withstand the strong tension and burst open. Like springs, each of the flaps throws the seeds from their beds for distances of up to several metres. The strong pressure is induced by a quantity of sugar solution in the cells of the tissue. When ripe, the pods are under enormous pressure. Consequently the plant easily spreads, and can be found along forest paths, especially in damp undergrowth. Its southern Siberian companion, often as quickly spreading as a weed, is the *Impatiens parviflora.*

The fruits of the **Squirting cucumber** (*Ecballium elaterium*)

91

Touch-me-not, **shooting its seeds into its surroundings.**

work like a paint spray gun or a steam catapult. This is a creeping plant related to the cucumber, belonging to the family of *Cucurbitaceae.* It grows as a weed in the warm regions of the Mediterranean. The soft stem, heart-shaped leaf and yellow flowers look at first sight rather similar to a wild cucumber. However, the fruits are only 4—5 cm (1.5—2 in) long, plum-shaped berries, being thickly covered with bristles. They have an unbearably bitter taste.

When ripe, the fruit drops from its stalk. Within, there is a mixture of sticky juice and large brown seeds. There is an enormously high pressure inside the fruit, which eventually becomes so great that it bursts open, flinging the seed over an enormous distance. The range of the shot is said to be up to 12 m (39 ft), and the seeds are ejected at a speed of nearly 10 m/sec (32 ft/sec). The seeds are fired up at an angle of 50—55 degrees, which means they easily avoid such obstacles as the plant's own leaves. A relative, the South American *Cyclanthera,* 'shoots' in a similar way.

The flat fruits of the African succulent *Dorstenia* have a much lower pressure. The first seed is expelled like slippery soap from a wet hand to a distance of about 1 m (3 ft), then as the pressure drops further seeds merely slip out and fall to the ground.

A Light Construction

It is not only trees that tower over us — plants do so as well. Perennial grass, the **Bamboo** (*Bambusa*), for example, has woody stems up to 40 m (131 ft) high. In a bamboo jungle, an elephant will be as small as an ant in a flower bed.

Bamboo is a tropical grass. It grows the fastest of all dry land plants, 70 to 100 cm (27—39 in) a day. It shares first place in the world for speed of growth with the rapid-growing brown seaweed, which achieves a final length of 50—65 m (160—213 ft).

Bamboo is most important in its native lands, China, Japan and India, and also in those countries to which it is exported as a raw material. It is a very suitable building material. Its hollow stems are remarkably strong, light and long lasting, thanks to the smooth, strong surface.

Bamboo is used to make support columns and beams for homes, simple flexible bridges, rafts, the masts and yard arms of boats, musical instruments, fences, walking sticks, and handles for tools. Split strands are used to weave mats, baskets,

Squirting cucumber **and its exploding fruit.**

A Bamboo **thicket**.

Bamboo **is the common building material in Guinea.**

roofs and the partition walls of dwellings. The list of uses is endless. And do not forget the young bamboo shoots. Not only are they a favourite treat for elephants and pandas, but they also make delicious meals for humans.

Armed to the Teeth

When early man went hunting, he knew that a blow to the head, using a blunt instrument, could kill an animal or an enemy. But he soon learned from nature that a sharp, pointed weapon had much greater advantages, and could be more dangerous and useful when it came to cutting up meat. One inspiration could well have been the thistle, with its sharp bristles.

More than one **Thistle** (*Carduus*) is well equipped for life, as are other related or similar plants. The plant is protected against plant-eating animals because it is prickly and poisonous. Although they eat everything in sight, including branches, the thistle is completely ignored.

Very similar thistles and teasels are differentiated according to the down on top of the plant. In the teasle the down is like feathery bristles, while the thistle is crowned with down composed of simple hairs.

A vigorous, even bizarrely shaped plant is the **Scotch Thistle** (*Onopordon acanthium*) which is entirely covered with greyish woolly felt. The stems are broadly winged and bristled.

The giant panda, listed among the endangered species, is an inhabitant of bamboo forests where it lives on young bamboo stems and leaves.

93

The Thistle.

The Scotch thistle.

Thistles **and** teasels **protect themselves from being plucked or grazed with their** prickles. Similarly, the iron armour of mediaeval knights and their horses had many spikes and sharp edges for protection during battles and tournaments. The most menacing were the points on their hand weapons *(below)*.

Two Sides of the Same Coin

Another unpleasant plant is the **Stinging nettle** (*Urtica dioica*). Not only is it an obstacle to people walking through open woods and across wasteland but it has also spread into gardens and parks. Its presence among weeds is always betrayed by its sharp 'sting'.

The stinging hair is an excellently constructed mechanism. The base narrows into a thin needle ending with a blunt point and a hooked protrusion. The slightest touch causes the hooked end to break off, whereupon the sharp 'hypodermic' tube pierces the skin and allows a small amount of liquid to enter. The liquid is a protein, similar to snake venom!

However, this disagreeable plant also has many useful properties. Extracts from stinging nettles are used in cosmetic creams and shampoos, and as a food colouring. Nettles also contain many valuable vitamins, and were once cooked like spinach.

Stinging nettles have been useful in other ways too, and can be

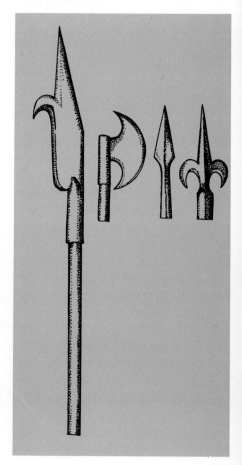

spun to form a reasonable cloth. Although the nettle fibres are fragile and easily break, they provide

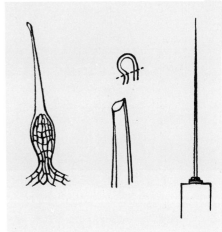

The hairs on the Stinging nettle *(left)* are like small hypodermic syringes *(above)*. On contact with the skin the rounded head of the hair breaks off, the sharp edges penetrating the flesh like a hypodermic syringe. An unpleasant fluid is injected into the skin, causing a red lump, similar to a burn mark.

a fine, soft yarn. The one problem, of course, is that the material can irritate the skin. For this reason, the use of stinging nettles for weaving cloth has been restricted only to times of emergency!

The **Common elder** (*Sambucus nigra*) is a rather more friendly plant. There is an old saying, which few weeds can boast, about the elder: 'Take your hat off to the chamomile but kneel to the elderberry.'

People used to plant the bush near cowsheds because it was believed that it would drive away cattle plague. But it was also thought that the elder gave shelter to awesome evil spirits because of its un-

pleasant smell. For this reason, people did not like digging up the bush lest they angered the spirits.

In the Tyrol it was claimed that 'the elderberry is more precious than gold because all of it is curative.' From time immemorial, all parts of the elderberry have been used in folk medicine and in modern times in pharmacy. In June and July the flower heads bloom richly with creamy flowers that spread around themselves their special, unique smell. This fragrance is not lost, even when the flowers are used to make lemonade, syrup, or refreshing tea, or when the flower heads are coated in batter and fried! The black,

seedy berries help people to empty their bowels and bladder, and soothe inflamed nerves.

The juice is used to make wine, and was earlier used to dye cloth and to colour small statues of sacred gods. The fruits, with their rich content of vitamins, acids and sugars, are processed into jams and jellies. It is also possible to make a brew from the leaves, roots and bark. Finally, the bark of young twigs can heal burns, and toothaches be relieved with a splinter of elderberry wood. All these uses make the elderberry one of the finest medicinal plants in existence.

A Sensitive 'Instrument'

A lichen is not one organism but two, the fungus and alga. They complement each other and present themselves as one whole plant. The fungus provides the water supply, drawing it in through its entire surface, at times only in the form of water vapour or fog. Yet this is enough for the lichens. The

Common elder.

substances or pollution in the air. This also applies to rain water which, on its way down through the air, picks up the sulphur dioxide from the smoke of chimneys, and combines with it to make sulphurous acid which is very poisonous to the tissues of lichens.

The lichen, *top far right,* **Icelandic moss** (*Cetraria islandica*), grows on the ground, either singly or in groups. For several centuries it has been used in folk medicine. Fortunately, it does not belong to the lichens that have entirely disappeared from many high mountainous regions, such as the *Usnea*. Their bushily branched, thread-like bodies now hang from the branches of trees like patches of dense hair. One of the few places where they can still be found are in the National Park of

Elderberry **was the base of many medicines in old dispensaries, the forerunners of today's chemists.**

green algae use the water and carbon dioxide from the air to create organic substances with which they also feed the filaments. Both of them play an equal part in reproducing. The lichen releases a cluster of fungal filaments and algae, which develop into new lichen.

Lichens contain a quantity of acids which eat away at the surface of bare rocks. But while they are not too fussy about a comfortable location, they are very sensitive to atmosphere. This makes them excellent indicators of pollution in the atmosphere, and where this occurs they disappear from afflicted areas. But there are species now known today that are adaptable, and are even spreading in such polluted areas.

Only part of the dual organism of lichens is green, which is why they grow and generate very slowly. But in growing slowly they are particularly liable to poisonous

Lichen of the *Usnea* family.

Icelandic moss.

A schematic cross-section of a lichen thallus: (a) The skin, or the fungal part, (b) The algal layer, (c) Fungal hyphae, (d) The bottom of the thallus, (e) Rhizines.

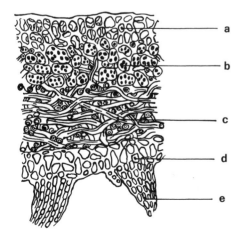

the Pyrenees and in the Caucasus, by the Black Sea.

Caoutchouc Conquering the World

One of the plants that has played an important part in pushing forward the development of technology is, without doubt, the **Brazilian caoutchouc** (*Hevea brasiliensis*).

It was in quite recent times — at the end of the last century — that caoutchouc became prized for its supplies of latex, which was made into rubber. However, the Mexican Indians had known about this for some time, and had been using the latex to make balls for sports and games.

The Brazilian rubber tree grows wild along the Amazon River and, up to 1875, brought great wealth to Brazil from the sale of raw caoutchouc all over the world. It was not at all easy to seek out the trees scattered through the impenetrable jungle, to cut them, obtain

the white latex and bring it out. The collector proceeds by making a V-shaped cut in the bark of the tree, and repeats this after two or three days. It takes 30—40 cuts to obtain 1 litre (0.2 gallon). The juice hardens at once and is dried over a fire.

Although the Brazilian government tried for a long time to prevent rubber trees being taken and grown outside its area, the English succeeded in taking several thousand seeds of the plant to Malay and Borneo. The tree flourished in similar climatic conditions, though in large plantations it was more susceptible to disease.

First products made from rubber were very imperfect. From 1811, Vienna was producing rubber tubing, shoes, rain coats and india rubber for office use. And then, in the middle of the 19th century an American inventor, Charles Goodyear (1800—1860), enriched caoutchouc with sulphur. This gave the rubber added strength. It no

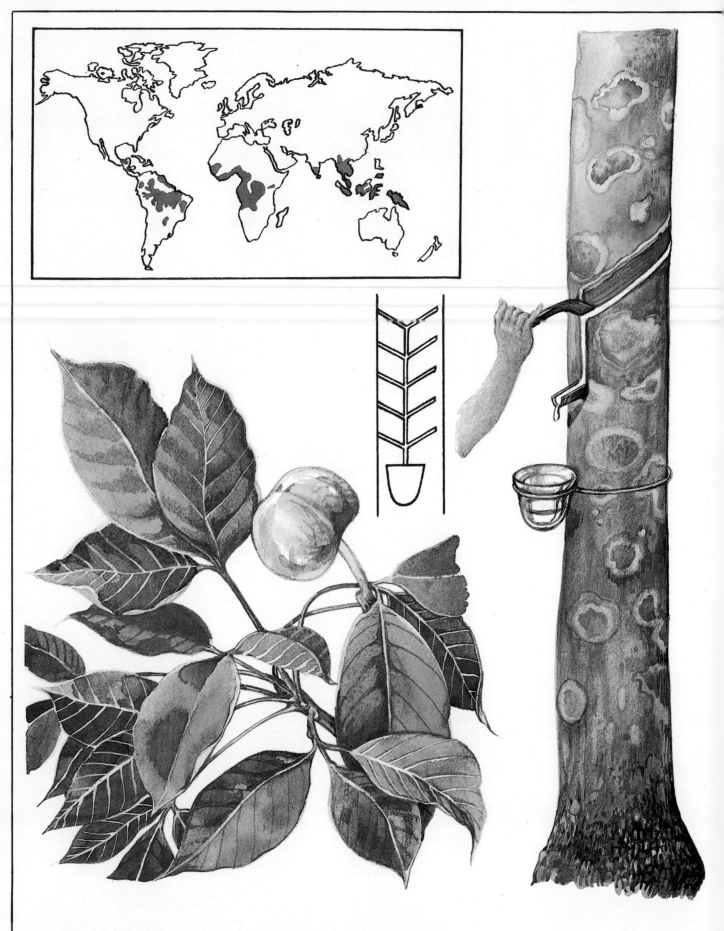

The use of caoutchouc as an industrial raw material is a fairly recent event, coming at the end of the last century.

Top left: **A map showing the cultivation of** Brazilian caoutchouc.
Above: **A small branch with its seed.**

Right: **Collecting latex by cutting the bark of trees.**

longer broke easily and was not sticky, and became ideal for cyclists' shoes and car tyres. Caoutchouc is now produced artificially from crude oil or natural gas which contains carbons similar to caoutchouc.

The tyres of an old car.

VI PLANTS, ART AND ARCHITECTURE

Since time immemorial man's life has been closely connected with plants. For this reason, ancient cultures highly valued plants and revered some of them as sacred. Proof of this has come with findings in old tombs. Flowers, which delighted man, were cultivated in gardens, despite their passing beauty. Of much greater permanence is the beauty of flowers, caught by the brush and paints of the artist on canvas, paper, plaster, or engraved on stone, wood, glass, porcelain and precious metals. These flowers endure for centuries. An excellent example are the bright meadows covered with roses, cornflowers, mignonette, and wild poppy, painted on the ceilings of churches at the end of the 18th century in Hungarian villages and in many other places.

An enthralling masterpiece of present day flowers can be seen on the historic square Grande Place in Brussels. A vivid 1,600 sq m (17,222 sq ft) carpet, depicting the colourful historic emblems of Brussels is composed of hundreds of thousands of dahlias and begonias.

Walter Crane's illustrations for the book *Flowers from Shakespeare's Garden* **(London, 1905).**

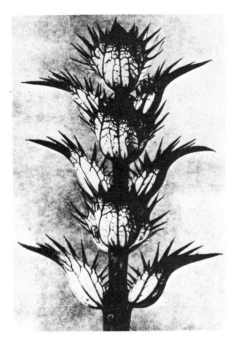

The elegant leaf shape of the *Acanthus mollis.*

An example of mediaeval ornamentation. Fabulous animals were frequently used to illustrate manuscripts from the 2nd half of the 14th century onwards.

The Art of the Leaf

From ancient times up to the Middle Ages, the leaf of the thistle **Acanthus** has become a part of architecture and painting. The thistle belongs to the *Acanthaceae* family, which grow as plants or trees mostly in the tropics and sub-tropics, except for the more hardy species of the Mediterranean region (*Acanthus mollis*) and (*Acanthus spinosus*). The first has softly curling and prettily indented leaves, while the points of the leaves of the second group are divided and sharp, like those of the thistle.

The leaf was a popular artistic image for many centuries, being known to artists as an acanthus. We can see its image on very old buildings and in ornamental horizontal strips, placed at the top

An initial letter ornamented with Acanthus leaves and plant tendrils.

A Corinthian capital adorned with Acanthus leaves.

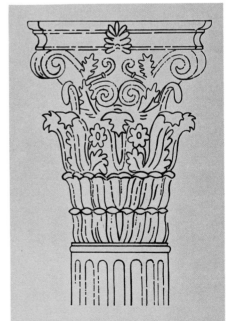

of slim supporting columns.

Acanthus leaves ornament mediaeval prayer and hymn books. They are used in many stone sculptures, artistic carvings, over doorways and entrances to palaces, on metal gratings and keys, and also as a decoration on gold jewelry, and later on porcelain.

Water Lilies

Water lilies (*Nymphaea*) have long been a fine source of inspiration both in art and architecture. They were cultivated in 'water gardens' as far back as the Hanging Gardens of Babylon (constructed c. 8th—6th century B.C.), and have been admired by the Greeks, the Romans and Hindus. The finest gardens of antiquity contained pools with fountains and water lilies.

The praises of the water lily were sung lyrically by the Chinese poet Chan Tun I: 'It has been a matter of fashion since the T'ang dynasty (since the year 608) to admire the beauty of the peony, but I like best of all the water lily. How it rises without blemish above its water flowerbed! How modestly it rests on the translucent pool — like

The Water lily on a lake in Japan.

A late 19th century Art Nouveau depiction of a Water lily.

a symbol of purity and truth!' The water lily is on pond or lake, as is a rose in the garden. Without doubt it is the queen of 'the watersprite's garden', and was believed by the Greeks to be a nymph changed into a magic flower.

Together with pondweed and the brandybottle lily, the water lily is the most typical and best-known water plant on the surface of pools, the dead arms of rivers and backwaters throughout Europe. They are often grown in various colours and sizes in water basins and pools, and in gardens and parks.

The flower's graceful shape made it very attractive to the artists at the end of the 19th century. They delighted in gentle, lightly flowing movements, as found in the plant's stem, the stalk, leaves

and flowers. They also adored the gracefulness of a swan's neck, peacock feathers, the fine bright autumn crocus, field poppies and

A stylized Yellowbottle lily in modern metal relief.

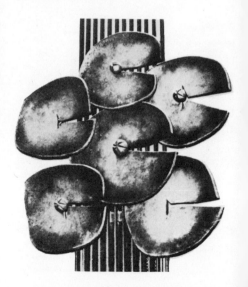

long lines of reeds. The artists used all these images to decorate dishes, glass goblets, jewels, the railings of balconies and stairways, and gables over entrances.

A less attractive relative of the water lily is the **Yellowbottle lily** (*Nuphar lutea*). Its fragrant flowers are like small, half-open barrels. However, the heart-shaped leaves are very attractive when reproduced on modern metal plastic art. Indeed, it was the metallic shine of its leaves that gave the yellowbottle lily its scientific name. It was derived from the Arab *naufar*, meaning blue shine.

The Egyptian **Lotus flower** (*Nymphaea lotus*), a white-flowered relative of the water lily, has for a long time been considered sacred. It grew on the banks of the Nile, whose waters and annual floods meant life for the dry Egyptian soil. This splendid, fragrant flower was so popular with the ancient Egyptians that is was frequently used as a model by painters, sculptors and builders. The lotus represented fertility, and was also a symbol of constantly returning life through the power of the gods. A small statue depicting the sun god in a lotus flower expresses the highest regard for the lotus and also for the life-giving light of the sun, the creative Deity.

Egyptian artists frequently depicted, in various ways, the birth of the sun from the lotus flower on carvings and bronze statues. The idea also influenced the Hindu religion. The idea then spread with the influence of Buddha to Tibet, and across China to Japan. The symbol of the Deity on a lotus throne also captured the interest of the Greeks at the time of the military campaigns of Alexander the Great (356—323 B.C.).

And so a great variety of deities and saints changed places on the Lotus throne. The inexhaustible image of the lotus then spread to the arts. It also had a vital influ-

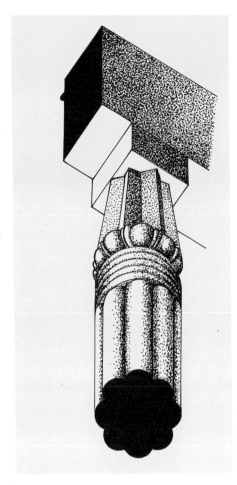

An Egyptian stone column with a Lotus flower design.

ence on both Asian religion and paintings, statues and architecture. The image of the lotus flower can also be found decorating columns and temple altars.

The quiet surfaces of tropical waters are covered by the largest of the water lilies — the *Victoria regia*. Its home is in South America, on the Amazon River. Travellers coming across it for the first time at the beginning of the last century were thrilled by what seemed to be a miracle. The splendour of its fragrant white flowers, more than 40 cm (16 in) across, was intensified by the size of the gigantic leaves, up to 2 m (6.5 ft) in diameter. The top is light green, the underpart purplish, and the edges are turned up. They grow very rapidly. This pampered jewel of glasshouses has a leaf growth of up to 3 cm (1.2 in) in an hour, and 30 cm (12 in) in a day! The circular leaves, like spacious trays, are so wide and strong that it is even possible for a small child to sit in them.

The basic construction of these leaves is a network of strong and markedly protruding rib-like veins.

The Sun god in a Lotus flower.

A network of veins is the weight-bearing construction of the gigantic leaves of the Victoria regia lily. This is a view of the underside of the leaf.

An English gardener, Joseph Paxton (1803—1865), made a daring plan for a glasshouse based on the principle of the weight-bearing construction of the leaf. In its time, it was thought to be one of the architectural wonders of the world. The masterpiece, called the Crystal Palace, was 563 m (1,848 ft) long, 124 m (406 ft) wide and covered an area of 70,000 sq m (753,480 sq ft). It was built in just six months for the World Exhibition held in London in 1851.

This astonishing work of so-called metal architecture was constructed of 3,300 cast iron pillars, 2,224 cross beams, and 205,000 wooden frames to hold 300,000 panes of glass. It was something absolutely new. The vaulted roof of the building was a copy of the firm but light network of the leaf veins of the *Victoria regia*. When the exhibition ended, the Crystal

The inspiration for the technical wonder of its time, the splendid glasshouse called the Crystal Palace, were the huge leaves of the Victoria regia lily. The firm, flat blade of the leaf is reinforced by a network of protruding veins so strong that the leaf can even bear the weight of a moderately large child. The vaulted roof of the spacious glasshouse, built for the World Exhibition in 1851, was also extremely strong.

Palace was dismantled and moved to Sydenham where it stood until 1936, when it was destroyed by fire.

The rounded dome of the Small Palace of Sport, built in Rome (1958—59) and designed by the architect Pier Luigi Nervi, also calls to mind *Victoria regia.* The reinforced ribs cross each other and form a network of square sections which strengthen the dome, built of thin reinforced concrete.

Palm Metamorphoses

Palms are one of the most useful plants, and naturally grow in the tropics. They are a tremendous natural source of nutrition, and offer a variety of materials for daily use and ornament. The close relationship between man and palms extends throughout the arts and technology.

A characteristic feature of palm trees are their regular, fan-shaped leaves. The Europeans have imported the palm, and refer to the ornamental patterns on their leaves as *palmetto.* Palmettos were used as ornamental motifs in European architecture from the 12th to the 19th century.

A new solution for a self-supporting roof construction has been found by architects, taking the palm tree as an example. The group of palms with fan-shaped leaves includes the south Chinese and east Australian **Livistone Palm** (*Livistona australis*). The tall trunk, covered with a network of fibres, a residue after the falling of leaves, carries a mighty crown of leaves. Their stalks are spiny and the 1 m (3 ft) long blades are arranged into 40—50 pleats which are deeply cut inwards from the edges like a fan.

This simple manner of pleating the leaves greatly increases their strength. Engineers have adopted this principle when attempting to increase the strength of roofs, the bodies of aircraft, the walls of metal garages, the facings of balconies, and also corrugated cardboard for the packaging of easily damaged articles.

The idea of a self-supporting roof structure, based on the palm leaf, was applied for the first time in 1965 during the building of a covered entry to the Alpine road tunnel under Mont Blanc, which is one of the longest in the world.

Palms are plants that are ex-

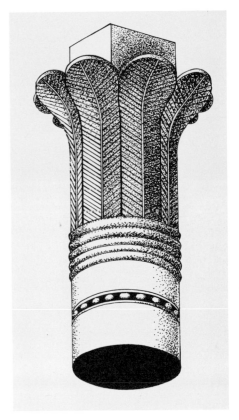

The palm-shaped capital of a column.

traordinarily useful and the **Coconut palm** (*Cocos nucifera*) is perhaps the most useful of all. The palm grows in the tropics, where almost every part of it is used. Some of the products and especially the fruit, the well-known 'nuts', are even sent abroad to people who, sadly, have never seen the magnificent, 50 m (165 ft) high, coconut palm.

After fertilization, the inconspicuous flowers in the top of the crown of leaves change into a heavy harvest of 10—30 nuts on each tree. The nuts are harvested up to four times a year. The fruit is a kernel concealed under the smooth, leathery skin. Its hard shell is overgrown with a dark layer. Inside is the white, hollow seed, filled with a sweetish, refreshing liquid, coconut milk.

The seed of the coconut palm is one of the largest in the world. It contains such a rich supply of nutrients that they can nourish the

An anthemion — a design based on flower shapes.

The nervure (or vein) of palm leaves.

The self-supporting construction of the covered entrance to the tunnel under Mont Blanc.

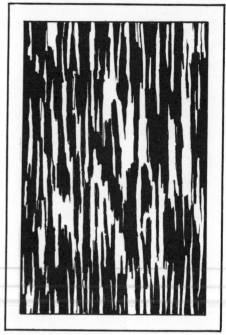

A lengthwise section of the wood of the coconut palm.

young plants for several years. The fruit provides a valuable oil, used for making margarines, soaps and cosmetics. The shells, with their dry fibrous layers, are soaked in order to obtain a raw material called coir. This is turned into a rough fabric used for making sacks, mats, carpets, and also brushes and ships' ropes which are resistant to salt water. Buttons are cut from the shells, the un-opened flower heads are used to make a sweet palm juice to be drunk directly, or are kept to pro-duce palm wine. It can even be made into syrup and brown sugar.

The most substantial part of the tree, the wood of the trunk and the huge leaves, become vital building materials. They give a characteris-tic look to the native buildings. The natives use the dry leaves as a roof covering and for weaving mats and baskets. The wood of the trunk is very durable and is used for the inner panelling of houses and for the production of orna-mental furniture. Because of the striped pattern of the wood it is re-ferred to as 'porcupine wood'.

A rare palm (*Lodoicea seychel-*

Palm leaves are used as a roof covering on native huts.

to negate any poisonous drinks poured into them.

Simplified out of Recognition

Under the ground the **Lily** (*Lilium*) has an oval bulb of overlapping fleshy scales. Above the ground is a stem carrying an abundance of foliage, the leaves being short and spear-shaped. The leaves of the *Iris* are very similar in shape, but they are stiff and attached at right angles to the stem, in two rows. The perennial part of the iris is the underground rhizome.

The flowers of the lily and the iris are almost identical in structure. There are two circles of three petals, but in the latter they bend in, while in the iris they curve backwards.

Both flowers, so lovely and well liked, have throughout history often been used for decoration and their images used by artists. However, when their images are simplified it becomes very difficult to tell them apart. And other flowers have also added to the confusion. So the lily of the Hebrews was not our lily but rather a white lotus, a rose, a narcissus or an iris. Similarly, the place of the lily in ancient Egypt was held by the water flower, the lotus. The Greeks and the Romans were acquainted with the lily. The Greek poet Homer called the white lily *leirion*, which comes from the word *leiroe*, meaning pale and delicate.

How does this botanical confusion show itself in the arts? Architects used drawings of plants to decorate columns in buildings. However, the tops of huge columns shaped like lilies, which are the work of Phoenician builders of a great temple, are not copies of our lily but the flower of the lotus.

Coloured red and white, the lily also finds itself in the emblem of the Italian city of Florence. At the time of the mediaeval develop-

larum), grows on the Seychelles islands off the east coast of Africa. High above their lofty trunks they bear fruits similar to coconuts, but much larger — in fact they are among the largest tree fruits in the world. The fleshy seeds, concealed under the thin, stone-hard shell of the nut, are just as impressive. They are over 40 cm (15 in) long and weigh 10—15 kg (22—33 lb).

The large nuts containing the largest seed in the world develop from the small flowers of the palm, and they take seven years to ripen. The large nut is not carried away and scattered on the sea like the fruits of the coconut palm, because it is filled completely with the flesh of the seed. That is why this palm remains faithful to the islands whose name is carried in its scientific name.

People used to think that these nuts were born by palms under the sea, and that they floated up to the surface from the depths as 'sea nuts'. And in the Middle Ages drinking vessels were made from the shells, which were supposed

The nut of the Seychelles palm **contains the largest seed in the world, which can grow up to 40 cm (15 in).**

The flowers of the Madonna lily *(left)* **and the** Florentine lily *(right)*.

ment of trade, Florence became one of the world's most important trade centres with its own currency replacing that previously used by the Byzantines. The Florentine

The Iris **flower** *(top)* **has passed through many forms, artists often merging its image with that of the stylized Lily. Proof of this artistic freedom is the depiction of the Iris in heraldry** *(left)*. *Right:* **The upturned, stylized, Iris flower used as an architectural feature.**

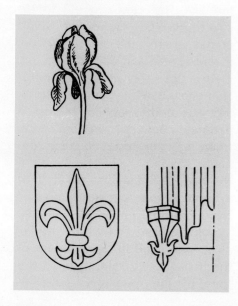

piece of gold bearing the picture of a lily was called *fiorino d'oro*, the little golden flower, or florin.

We find stylized lilies in heraldic signs, especially in France. The French always have directly worshipped this 'flower of flowers'. The lily decorated the sceptre of the first kings of France. The *fleron* at the end of the sceptre came to be known later as *fleur de lis*, the stylized 'lily flower', which was contained in the king's emblem from the 14th century and was also on his seal, on the embroidery of the royal robes and on tapestries.

There have been many occasions when the lily, simplified, appeared on the flag carried by the military crusades and on shields. During the reign of Louis XII (1498—1515) this favourite flower was elevated to become the national flower. It was a must in all gardens. And previously, in the Middle Ages, some rulers established military 'orders of the lily'. One of the last of them was the Order of the Lily founded by the Bourbon King Louis XVIII (1775—1824). The sign of the order

was a white silk ribbon bearing a silver lily. The lily was thus opposed to the violet of the Bonapartists.

A Wonderful Likeness

There are some buildings, such as the temples in the Indian town of Bhubaneshvar, and the Church of

An ancient Egyptian column carrying the motif of a stylized lily. On the *right* **is an outline of the column showing the stems of the lily in relief.**

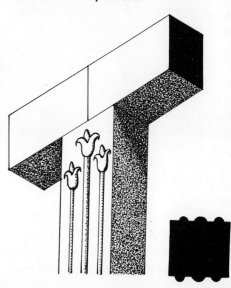

The famous Florentine gold piece *fiorino d'oro* (gold flower) carried on its opposite side the emblem of Florence — a lily. The coins were used in the Middle Ages from the mid-13th century.

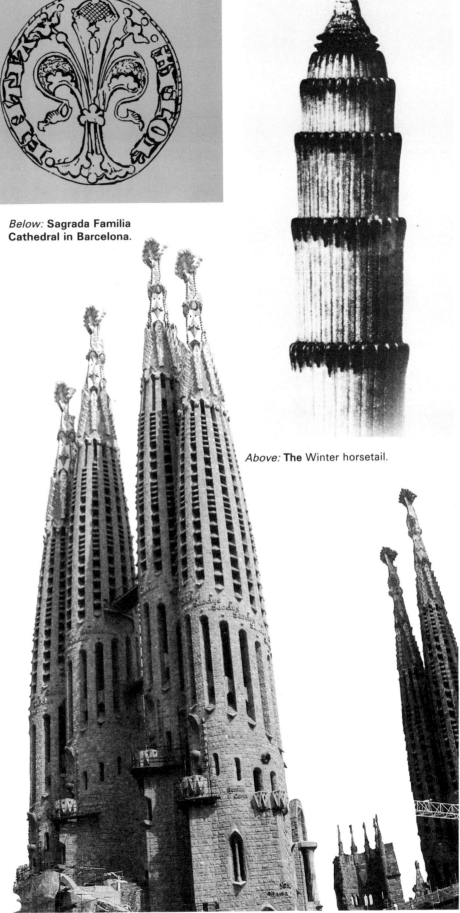

Below: Sagrada Familia Cathedral in Barcelona.

Above: **The** Winter horsetail.

the Holy Family in the Spanish town of Barcelona, that are utterly striking. The slender, rounded shapes of the buildings are markedly different from other buildings, and on close inspection reveal certain similarities to plants. It is as if the architects had studied the stems of one particular plant, the **Horsetail.**

The sturdy stems of **Winter horsetail** (*Equisetum hiemale*) stand stiff and straight. They persist through the winter for several years. They grow up to more than 1 m (3 ft) high, and have a rough skin. Only rarely does a cone of spores appear on top. It is formed of six-sided plates with a large quantity of spores inside.

The original concept of the Sagrada Familia cathedral in Barcelona is a creation of the unbounded fantasy of the excellent Spanish architect, constructor and artist, Antonio Gaudí (1852—1926). His work was influenced by the creative style of Art Nouveau (in the late 19th century), inspired by images of plants and animals.

Another daring and quite untraditional solution was presented by the architect of the American re-

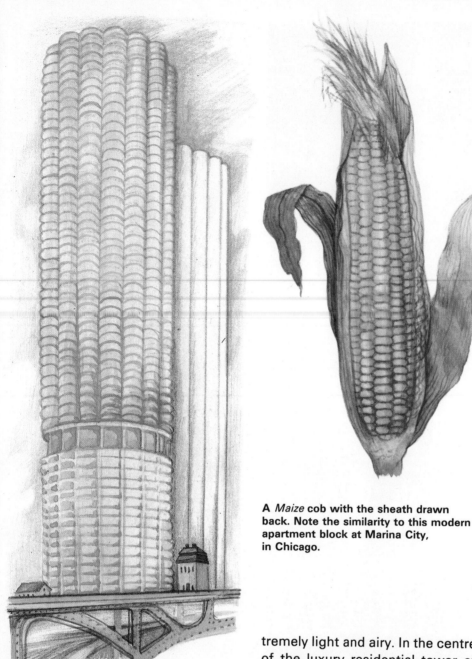

A *Maize* cob with the sheath drawn back. Note the similarity to this modern apartment block at Marina City, in Chicago.

later became popular among the people, too.

The god of wine was Dionysus, in whose honour there were many celebrations. Greek and Italian artists frequently depicted Dionysus in their paintings and statues. The plant vine is also a frequently used image in works of art. Its very long spiralling tendrils can be painted in such a way that they provide marvellous decoration round a scene, and they have even been copied when designing flower-beds. The tendril design also appears in the elegant curving of metal railings around the tombs of kings.

Porcelain is also sometimes decorated with the image of tendrils, leaves and bunches of grapes, producing an interesting elegant design.

We can see how far back the cultural history of the grape vine extends, for there is a sign for the vine in Egyptian hieroglyphics. As with the Chinese characters, there is one symbol for every word.

The Onion-like Peony

One of the most important centres for the production of porcelain is the German factory at Meissen. However, it was no overnight success. It took people a long time and cost a number of generations many sleepless nights to discover the secret of making the highest quality, thin Chinese porcelain. Before this discovery, at the beginning of the 18th century, there had only been imitation Chinese porcelain.

The Oriental style had also influenced the way the porcelain was decorated. It was a very popular custom to decorate articles of porcelain and whole dinner services with Chinese images, particularly flowers and birds. Most in demand in the middle of the 18th century was the Chinese blue design. It included scenes with bamboo, chrysanthemums, and the

tremely light and airy. In the centre of the luxury residential tower of 60 floors is a circular core containing lifts, stairways and corridors to the individual apartments. Each room narrows from the circumference to the centre, like a piece of cake which narrows to a point, or like the maize grain.

A Popular Motif

The **Wine grape** (*Vitis vinifera*) has been known from the oldest times because it bears juicy berries that provide an alcoholic drink — wine. This popular drink was sacred in ancient Egypt and could only be drunk by the priests, although it

sidential complex, Marina City, on the banks of Chicago Lake. The pair of circular high-rise apartment houses, designed by Bertrand Goldberg, dates from 1960—1965. The splendid buildings imitate the arrangement of grains on a cob of **Maize** (*Zea mays*). The open arrangement of this imaginative building makes the rooms ex-

A porcelain dish with a grape vine motif.

The sign for the grape vine in Egyptian hieroglyphics indicates a rich grape harvest.

Ornamental iron railings enclosing the royal tomb in St. Vitus Cathedral, Prague.

A vine leaf and a bunch of grapes in Arabic creative art.

queen of Chinese flowers, the **Peony** (*Paeonia*).

The design was adapted to European taste and was repeatedly drawn and simplified until the little branches and leaves, which originally turned alternately inwards and outwards, were intertwined over the whole area. At the same time, however, the delicate unopened bud of the peony turned into an ordinary onion!

And that is the history of the 'onion design' on porcelain, which is still extremely popular among the collectors and admirers of lovely objects.

Arabesques

The flowers of the **Winter cherry**

A Peony bud.

An onion-design applied to porcelain.

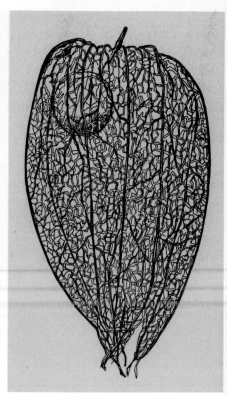

Inspiration from the Queen of Flowers

A few chance-selected specimens will remind us of the immensely

(*Physalis alkekengi*), with their white corolla, are very small. They look a little like the potato flower, and are also related to the Solanum family. However, after flowering, the calyx starts to grow and, while still green, encloses within itself the fruit, a berry of the size and colour of a reddish-orange cherry. It is not poisonous and its South American relative, *Physalis peruviana*, which has yellow berries, is even edible.

When mature, the enlarged, blown-up calyx is bright red. Because of its luminous colour and enchanting lantern shape, the plant is used in winter in dried floral arrangements without losing anything of its natural beauty. The feather-light lantern, covered with a thin skin, is so cleverly designed that the wind can easily carry its seed a considerable distance away from the parent plant. Eventually the blown up calyx turns into an attractive fine network of fibres which we find copied in the wall decorations of the Caliph's palace.

Cape gooseberry.

The network of veins on the gooseberry *(top left)* were the basis for the decorations in the Caliph's palace.

The rose motif is used in many different art forms. Illustrated here (from *top left*) are: historic rosettes; a porcelain pot with lid; the initial 'D' containing a rose; the opening petals of a metal rose; the emblem of the noble family of Rožmberk; and a tapestry purse.

stimulating and inspiring role of the **Rose** (*Rosa*).

Roses feature in many fairy tales, of which perhaps the best known is the Sleeping Beauty. The rose is also very important in many poems and in folk songs.

The natural beauty of the flowers even led people to use them as a pattern for their coats of arms, and guild signs, when decorating coins, metal and porcelain, and for painted glass and church windows. Roses also decorated the borders of the religious texts in mediaeval prayer books. Artists too were impressed by the rose, and many great masters use the flower to emphasize the harmony of colour or to underline the beauty of the scene. Roses from the garden and wild roses, together with other flowers, were of particular interest to artists at the end of the 19th century when the painting of floral subjects was at its height. Pierre Auguste Renoir (1841—1919) is looked upon as the king of floral painting. His work reflects his words that 'A picture must be a kindly, joyful or thrilling entity. There are enough unpleasant things in life without we ourselves making more!'

A Palette of Paints

Although many dyes are now

produced artifically, it is not very long since all dyes were natural, made from plants or animals.

One of the oldest plant dyes, golden-brown henna, comes from the oriental bush *Lawsonia inermis.* In ancient times henna was used to colour hair, beards, eyelashes and nails, as is evident from relics found in tombs. With **Indigo**, the strong blue dye of *Indigofera tinctoria,* we get a brown to black colour. Henna was also used to dye skins and fabrics.

Indigo, which gives a blue colour, is a tropical plant with red flowers. Long before the birth of Christ, the indigo plant was grown in the Orient, in Africa, and in southern Asia. The dye was obtained by soaking the fresh plant in water. Gradually, the dye settled

Indigofera tinctoria.

114

on the bottom of the vessel and was then taken out, dried and pressed into lumps. Indigo was then exported to Europe mainly from India as Bengalese indigo. From the 17th century on, it replaced in Europe a dye obtained from the leaves of **Woad** (*Isatis tinctoria*).

Indigo was mainly used for the production of the well-known 'blue' used in washing clothes and for dyeing cotton and linen used to make dresses, aprons, and so on. Indigo was also used to make special blue-white fabric, the 'blue print'.

It is very easy to put the pattern on the cloth. A shaped wooden object is brushed with a layer of starch and the pattern is printed onto the cloth. The cloth is then dyed in a cold bath of blue indigo. The whole piece turns blue except for the white design. This is a very old technique, known for centuries both in the Orient and in Europe, where the dye was sent.

Indigo became extremely popular in Europe in the 16th century, the Dutch being the first to copy this method of printing from the Persians. In the 17th century, the blue material with the white printed pattern took the fancy of the French royal court. It became a European fashion, as had imported Chinese porcelain with its blue and white pattern. The blue-print material was sometimes also called the 'porcelain print'.

The manufacture of blueprint.

VII A DECEPTIVE LIKENESS

Plants, like humans, have learnt how to be deceptive. But for the former it is often vital if they are to survive.

Masters of Deception

Orchids are the largest group of flowering plants, and there are more than 20,000 species throughout the world. Some orchids entice the insects that pollinate them with a delicate perfume, others by a foul smell, or with the striking colour and strange shape of the flowers.

Lady's slipper (*Cypripedium calceolus*) is one of the loveliest ground orchids of the temperate zone of Europe and Asia. In places it still grows wild, in deciduous woods and on bushy slopes, from May to June. It is, however, getting more and more rare as it is a victim of its striking appearance. Too many people collect them, though in many countries the wild orchid is a protected species. It grows throughout most of Europe, and eastward across the Caucasus and Mongolia to China and Japan and North America.

The strangely-shaped flower of lady's slipper measures about 5 cm (2 in). Under the maroon sepals is a striking pale yellow section, marked with dark lines on the outside and red spots inside. It is similar to a slipper, hence the plant's name.

The flowers of lady's slipper are very deceptive, because visiting insects will not find any food inside them. For they are, in fact, a trap.

Once inside, the bees slip down the flowers' smooth edges into the bottom. The insect is unable to climb back out the way it came, but is instead enticed to crawl over the hairs at the base of the labellum and around the anthers, where the pollen sticks to its back. The insect now flies off through another opening and when visiting another flower leaves the pollen, so fertilizing the seed.

The pollinated flower forms a seed which only rarely germinates in nature. The seed needs to come into contact with a fungus on which it is dependent for organic food in the first years of growth. The growth of a plant from seed takes a very long time, from 9 to 15 years. The erect stem of the plant carries 3—4, ribbed,

Cross-spider orchid.

Bumble bee orchid.

Ophrys insectifera.

The beautiful orchid, Lady's slipper.

doing so, carries pollen from one flower to another.

The remarkable family of the Ophrys is now extremely rare in the wild. They are among the most important orchids in Europe, especially southern Europe. They also grow in parts of North Africa and southwest Asia. The whole family comprises about 35 species.

An Attractive Odour

How surprised Dr. Arnold must have been when, on August 20th 1820 in Sumatra, he discovered a mysterious plant which still carries his name — *Rafflesia arnoldi.*

In the gloom of the interwoven branches and vines of the tropical forest, where everything is mouldering and decaying in the damp and warmth, the largest of all flowers blooms on the ground. It measures about 1 m (3 ft) across, and weighs from 5—8 kg (11—17 lb).

The plant is a parasite. Its body, which is restricted to sucking fibres, is immersed in the roots and branches of its host which is the *Cissus angustifolia,* a vine type plant. Only the flowers, which the local people call the devil's goblet, bloom on the ground. From the growth of a bud to the fading of the flower it takes three months. The conspicuous flower with brick-red coloured petals is covered with warts. In addition to its striking appearance there is an astonishing odour emitted by the flower to attract its pollinators. The flower smells like a piece of rotting meat. Insects are attracted by the smell of decay and carry away pollen to pollinate flowers of the opposite sex.

Other, much smaller flowers, such as the **Stapelias** *(Stapelia),* also emit the awful smell of rotting meat to attract flies. The flower's unusual appearance can also be

bright green leaves. From their centre grows a stem up to 50 cm (19 in) tall with one single, or sometimes two flowers.

One of the most perfect tricks in nature concerns the flowers of the orchid. They look exactly like the insects that pollinate them. Thus the **Bumble bee orchid** (*Ophrys fuciflora*) pretends to be a bumble bee; *Ophrys apifera* resembles a bee; *Ophrys arachnoidea* a cross-spider; and *Ophrys insectifera* a fly or a small wasp. The curious shape of the flowers represent the peak of specialization in plants which, in their flowers and their scent, imitate the female of the pollinating insect. The male insect flies around the plant and settles on what it thinks is the female, but is in fact the plant, and, in

Rafflesia arnoldi.

The flower of the Devil's goblet.

tion by insects. The florets bloom gradually from the circumference in towards the centre. The buds of the tubular flowers open and push out first of all the dark anthers holding the pollen. They attract bees which are usually busily seeking sweet nectar. The bees suck the juice and wipe themselves against the pollen. Further on they find the flowers that bloomed earlier, nearer to the edges. Their stamens have lost their pollen, and so they have prepared their styles and stigmas ready to accept the pollen from the young flowers.

The bee that visited the tubular flowers containing nectar and gathered pollen on its body, runs

The image of the Sunflower was particularly attractive to the artist Van Gogh.

observed by those who grow indoor plants. The stapelia flourishes on windowsills and often blooms in May. However, beware its unusual odour, especialy in the evening. Flies are sometimes so fooled by this odour that they lay eggs on the flower thinking it to be a piece of rotting meat.

When is a Flower Not a Flower?

The golden disc looks like a splendid flower on top of the thickly leaved stem. But it is not. It is a great cluster of small florets. The **Sunflower** (*Helianthus annuus*) can be up to 0.5 m (1.5 ft) across and is made up of about 1,000 small florets. The centre of the tiny, yellow-brown, tube-like florets is encircled with yellow, tongue-shaped florets. The centre flowers are fertile but the outer florets are infertile. They are the signals that attract pollinating insects to land.

The tiny florets, grouped together in what seems to be a single flower, 'co-operate' in the pollina-

Part of the flower head *(right)* **and the seed pods of the** Sunflower *(above).*

across the capitulum and inadvertently transfers pollen to the prepared stigmas, pollinating the flowers.

Nectar is no longer formed when the flower is not pollinated by insects. Self-pollination then takes place by the stigma turning over to contact its own pollen.

The regular arrangement of the florets can be better seen when the corollas have dropped off, and the black-white paving of seeds, gradually ripening from the edge to the centre, are visible.

The sunflower is such a great sun lover that its flowers can be seen turning their faces to the sun as it slowly moves across the sky. The sunflower is also interesting as one of the most useful cultivated plants. The plant was grown by the ancient Indians, but did not leave its Mexican homeland until 1510 when it was brought to Europe by the Spaniards. The Europeans bred this originally ornamental flower to become an immensely productive oil-plant.

The **Carline thistle** (*Carlina acaulis*) is a delightful work of art. Its ornamental rosette of leaves is spread out on the ground as if made of beaten metal. The light-coloured centre of the plant, and its flowers, is surrounded by silvery-white radiating bracts. They surround the capitulum, comprising a quantity of yellowish, red-tipped tubular florets. The yellowish capitulum contrasts with the outer dark green leaves, which are spiny, as are all the leaves of the carline thistle.

The carline thistle has a tough and spiny surface enabling it to survive on the dry bare slopes and wasteland where it grows, and also to protect it from grazing animals. This does not protect it from natural destruction, though, and in many European countries it is now a protected species.

In the centre of the spiny defence there is a wonderful crisp stalk with a flavour like cabbage. It is also used as a bathing solution to treat some skin diseases, and powder from the crushed root of the plant is used in veterinary medicine, stimulating the appetite of cattle. It was known in ancient times that the root of this thistle was curative, when it was called 'the root of the wild artichoke'.

Its spiny character, like that of the teasel, has meant that both plants are referred to as a **Thistle** (*Carduus*). This is perhaps also reflected in the Latin name *Carlina*. There are some who think the name of the plant was taken from the name of Charles the Great, to whom an angel was said to have appeared, telling him that the use

The Carline thistle.

119

of this plant would protect his troops against the plague.

What we take to be flowers in marsh marigolds, cuckoo-pints and many other of the 2,000 species of the order of *Araceae*, are not flowers at all. In fact they are the brightly coloured sheaths protecting the tiny flowers within.

The cornet-like sheath of the **Cuckoo-pint** (*Arum maculatum*) is whitish, greenish or even red-tinged, and mottled maroon inside. The large area and colourfulness of the sheath attracts pollinating insects to approach the inconspicuous flowers in the shade of the undergrowth of deciduous woods. Small insects are also drawn by the plant's odour. Inside the sheath, the insect is additionally attracted by the warmth because it is usually up to 15°C (59°F) warmer than outside. It feeds on the nectar of the male flowers. The insect flies about within the sheath, pollinating the flower. It spends up to two days there before the anthers ripen and the hairs enclosing the mouth of the interior droop and permit the pollen-carrying insect to leave. The fly escapes, seeks a warm place against the cold of the night in another flower, and the process starts over again.

The flowers of the separated sexes are crowded onto the spike at the centre of the plant (the spadix). The female flowers, and the stigmas, are at the bottom, resembling a swarm of bees on a branch. In a circle above them are the neatly arranged male flowers with the anthers. Both flowers are bare, lacking petals and sepals. The grouping ends with a brush of sterile flowers. The end of the spadix is rounded and without flowers.

In the spring the cuckoo-pint grows rapidly, flowers, and later the leaves wither. Only then does the fruit, consisting of fleshy red berries, ripen. The spadix and the

The Cuckoo-pint.

The cross-section of the sheath of the Cuckoo-pint.

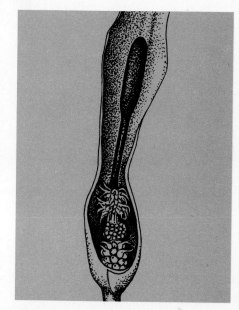

large, shining, green, spear-shaped leaves and the stalk of the sheath, all grow from a massive rhizome. The entire plant is poisonous, especially the rhizome. Even so, people used to cook the starchy rhizomes and then grind them into flour.

Complicated Conditions

The large family of the **Spurges** (*Euphorbia*) is spread almost throughout the world. They have an interesting, complicated arrangement of flowers which, at first sight, resembles a single flower. The female flower has a round ovary and three stigmas. It is on a long stalk and is surrounded by the male flowers. The whole group of flowers is protected by a number of bracts. They are conspicuous, yellow to red in colour, as a replacement for petals which are missing from the tiny flowers.

The imitation flower provides golden nectaries for the pollinating insects. The fruit is a warty pod containing three seeds. The seeds are equipped with a juicy appendage, a meal for the ants which then carry the seed away from the mother plant.

The delicate **Meadow grass**

(*Poa annua*) is one of a group of plants numbering several thousands which we class together as grasses. It has given its name to the whole order *Poaceae*. Apart from a few exceptions, they have a fairly simple construction. Over a bunch of fine roots grows a hollow stem, strengthened by a number of solid joints.

The simple little flowers are contained in spikelets, one on each (cat's tail grass) or more (meadow grass). The spikes form the inflorescence — the panicle. It is sometimes spread (meadow grass, spear grass) and sometimes closed (cat's tail grass). The tiny bisexual flowers have long filaments and pistils with striking stigmas. Instead of a calyx and corolla

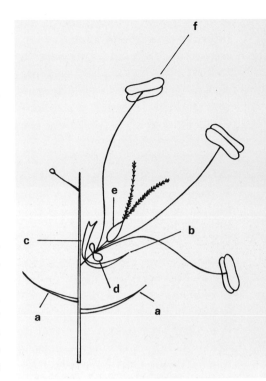

Spike of grass. (a) Blades (b) Glumes (c) Culm (d) Lemmas (e) Stigma (f) Anthers.

A Spurge. (a) Seed box (b) Part of the flower cluster (c) A cross-section.

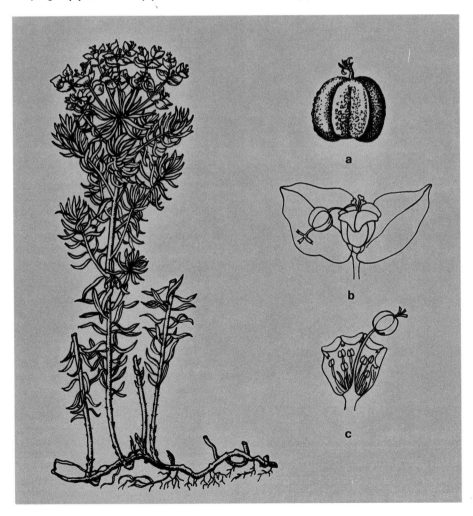

the flowers are protected by a larger awn and smaller skin-like awns. The whole spike is usually supported by two husks. The fruit is a grain. The pericarp is firmly attached to the seed case giving the wrong impression that it is a seed.

Meadow grass is very hardy, and starts to grow the moment frosts are less severe. A few warm days are enough. It even flowers before the onset of spring. Before winter it has formed up to three generations.

A Single Likeness

Just because two plants look like each other, does not mean that they are related. This is confirmed by a large group of plants described as **succulents**, derived from the Latin *succus*, meaning juice. They are plants with thick juicy stems, leaves, and roots, and store water in their fibres for times of drought. In dry places their

121

organs change to adapt to the difficult conditions. This means that even unrelated plants begin to look like each other. For example you might think you were looking at the fleshy column of a cactus when it is only a similar looking stapelia or ragwort.

Many plants reveal their true selves at the time of flowering. This is true of lithops, 'the living stone' of the desert, whose colour helps it to merge in with the surrounding stony ground. And we can easily recognize a 'cactus-like' spurge by making a small wound in the plant. White milk will immediately flow out of it.

Euphorbia obessa is a spurge which is more or less spherical and is divided up by shallow, almost undefinable ribs. The grey-green surface carries brownish stripes. *Lophophora williamsii* is a Mexican cactus with a soft spherical body free of thorns. It has a thick turnip-like root. *Astrophytum asterias* is one of the most peculiar of the Astrophytes, 'a star among cacti', highly prized by its many collectors.

The ball-shaped body has eight shallow ribs without thorns, covered with small white spots. *Aztekium* is a globular cactus with a number of ribs. The wrinkling of its surface recalls the faces of Indians, after whom this family of Mexican cacti has been named.

Stapelia has short fleshy stems which are branched and have four, roughly teethed edges. The curious flower is shaped like a star and resembles a piece of rotting meat. *Stapelia hirsuta* has flowers that are wrinkled and hairy. The flat seeds with long, fine hairs are spread across its South African homeland by the wind. The African species of *Senecio stapeliaeformis* has bare, fleshy stalks thrust upwards, with flat leaves at the top which later fall off. Their hard remnants are like thorns. The spurge *Euphorbia mammillaria*

comes from South Africa. It forms small branched plants with cylindrical, four-ribbed, 3—5 cm (1—2 in) thick stems, which are also divided into separate sections. The flower blooms at the top of a stalk, which remains after the flower fades, hardening into a thorn.

Another succulent is the South African *Pelargonium tetragonum*. The light green, smooth and angular little branches are around 7 mm (0.2 in) thick and fleshy. The circular leaves with wavy edges fall in the autumn. The plant grows into a semi-bush up to 70 cm (27 in) high. The long stem-like flowers are pink with purple stripes. A similar spurge, the *Euphorbia aphylla*, grows on the Canary Islands. It has long, thickly branched stems. The grey-green branches carry small round leaves at the top which drop off very early.

A group of plants with fleshy leaves arranged in a rosette has quite a different body. One example is the *Haworthia turgida* from the order *Liliaceae* from South Africa and the Cape. The fleshy, pointed leaves form a rosette. Similar plants are the South American *Echeveria*, from the order of the thick-leaved (*Crassulaceae*). It forms tufts of rosettes of various shapes and density on stalks. **Houseleeks** (*Sempervivum*) and **Stonecrops** (*Sedum*) with their many species, represent the succulents in the cooler regions of Europe. The east Mexican cactus *Ariocarpus trigonus* also forms rosettes of up to 10 cm (4 in) in diameter. It has a broad and thick turnip-like root in the ground. This is a cactus without thorns. Its yellow flowers bloom in great numbers in the axils of the 'leaves'.

Miniatures

Duckweeds are a small and sharply defined group of plants. They belong to those plants which

we call 'higher', though they are so small that they could easily be taken for algae. However, they make up for their negligible size by quantity. They often entirely cover a water surface like a green carpet, popularly known as 'a frog's lawn'. The duckweed has simplified its plant structure to the minimum. It lacks both stalks and a system for passing fluid through its body. It has only one green 'leaf' that floats on the water. *Lemna minor* and the humped *Lemna gibba* let down a single root from each section. The related *Spirodella polyrhiza* has a whole bunch of roots at the base of each section.

It is only a short step from duckweed to the smallest of all seed-bearing plants, the minute, rootless *Wolffia arrhiza* which is the simplest representative of the whole group of miniature plants. With a size of 1 mm (0.04 in) it could hardly find a rival for the record of the smallest plant, but it makes up for its insignificant size

A similarity of form does not always mean plants are related. This is demonstrated by a large group of plants called succulents. In the top row are three species of cacti: (2) *Astrophytum asterias*, (3) *Lophophora williamsii* and (4) *Aztekium*, which are similar in shape to (1) *Euphorbia obessa*.

In the second row are: (5) The Stapelia and (7) Huernia, which differ from the similar but unrelated (6) *Senecio stapeliaeformis* from the Asteraceae family only at the time of flowering.

In the third row is another Senecio (8) *Senecio articulatus* which is more like the succulent (9) *Pelargonium tetragonum* in shape, while the Spurge (10) *Euphorbia aphylla* is very like (11) *Rhipsalis salicornia*, a cactus from the *Rhipsalis* family.

The first rosette in the fourth row is the succulent (12) *Haworthia turgida*. (13) The Central American *Echeveria elegans* looks like the Central European succulent Houseleek (14). The final rosette is a cactus of the *Ariocarpus* family (15) *Ariocarpus trigonus*.

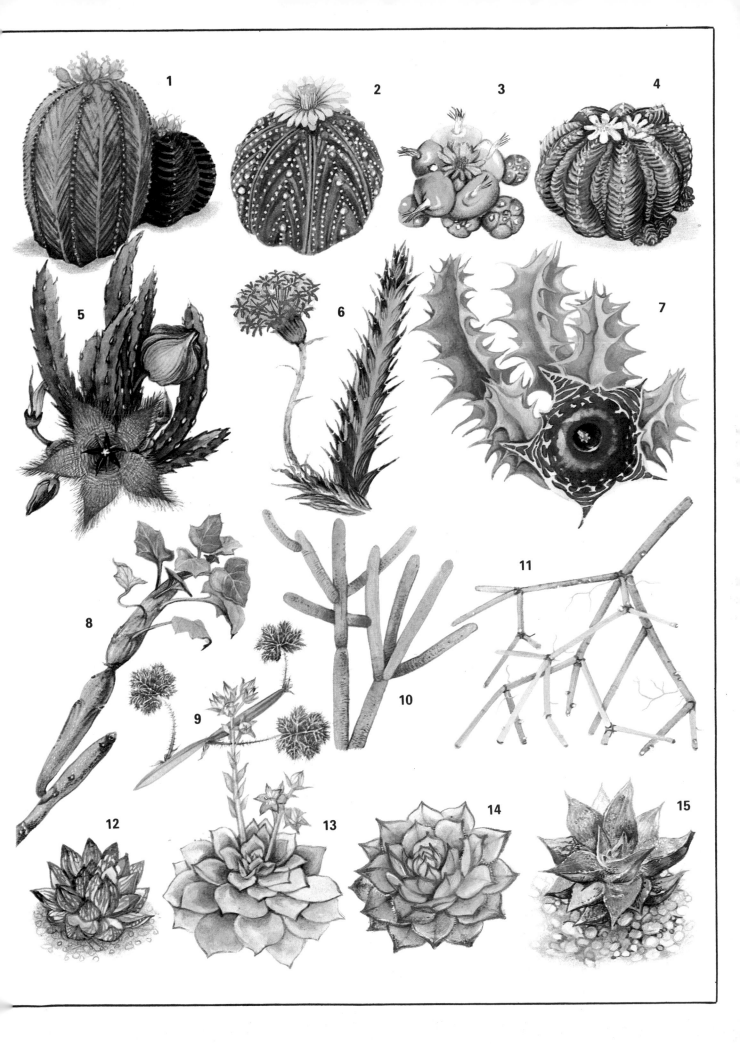

An old illustration of a monastery with a pool overgrown with duckweed.

Lemna minor.

by the speed of its propagation and growth. Although it rarely flowers, it has few problems in reproducing.

The mother section gives birth to young plants, or 'little leaves', from the side. Either they stay together or separate. They grow so quickly you can almost see it happening. Under good conditions, 26 hours are enough for the formation of a new plant. Given these facts, it is not surprising that we find these undemanding and vigorous plants in large quantities covering surfaces of pools, ponds, backwaters, marshes and stagnant waters right across the world.

124

VIII CHANGES IN LIFE STYLE

Plants are entirely independent and self-supporting. When a seed germinates, a new green plant seems to grow almost from nothing. We do not see that it is actually building its body from the carbon dioxide in the air, sunlight and water, together with other elements, which nourish the plant and keep it healthy.

It is such an every day occurrence that we rarely think what an extraordinary event this is. We call the life-giving process in plants photosynthetic assimilation. The process occurs in chlorophyll-filled plant cells. Carbon dioxide and water are changed, in the presence of light, into sugars and starch. In order to maintain a balance, the reverse process, dissimilation, also takes place, mostly at night time. During dissimilation, the disintegration of organic substances releases energy, oxygen is consumed, and carbon dioxide re-leased into the air. People do the same when breathing. They in-hale oxygen, and breathe out carbon dioxide.

▶ Plants are nourished by a process called photosynthetic assimilation, during which green plants turn simple mineral substances (carbon dioxide and water) into organic substances (sugars, starch). However, some of the water a plant draws in through its roots escapes into the atmosphere through the leaf blades.

Photosynthetic assimilation takes place in the presence of light, which is the source of energy for the process shown on the *right*. During photosynthesis plants take in carbon dioxide (CO_2) and give off oxygen (O_2). Photosynthetic assimilation ceases in the dark, when the plants breathe like humans, taking oxygen from the air and releasing carbon dioxide. The products of photosynthesis pass from the leaves to the roots.

A plant draws most of its nutrition from the soil through its roots. But in places with a poor supply of soil nutrients, especially nitrogen, the plant has to feed on something else.

Hunters of Live Prey

Some of the most interesting plants are those that are carnivorous (meat eaters). They have always attracted the interest of explorers and scientists, particularly Charles Darwin (1809—82), who made a study of the sundew. He wanted to discover whether the plant depended entirely on meat or only as a supplement to its diet. He discovered that though the sundew is a plant that is more pink than green in colour, it fares well on a meatless diet. It creates organic substances by photosynthetic assimilation. However, the meat-deprived plants are smaller, while those fed on meat are sturdier. On the poor, boggy soil, the sundew enriches its diet by eating insects.

If we look at the leaves of **Round-leaved sundew** (*Drosera rotundifolia*) against the sun, they sparkle as if set with gems. The sticky drops at the end of long hairs twinkle like morning dew. They are what the plant uses to catch its prey. Small insects settle on the sticky surface of the leaves, but become glued to it. As they struggle so the whole leaf gradually closes over its prey. The more the trapped insect struggles to escape, the more it finds itself caught in the plant's sticky tentacles. When the victim is finally secure, the hairs start to exude digestive juices. They break down the soft parts of the insect's body, which are then absorbed by the plant. The hard parts, such as the wings, are blown away by the wind and rain when the leaf re-opens. It takes the plant from several hours up to one day to absorb its catch.

One single sundew plant is able to consume as many as 2,000 insects, such as gnats, blight and flies, between the spring and autumn.

This quite small, nodding plant of the marshes has taken its place among the famous 'medicinal' herbs. The first mention of it dates back to the 13th century, after which it rapidly gained the reputation of having magic powers. It was used to cure persistent coughs, asthma, bronchitis and diabetes, as well as ailments of old age. Since there is a danger that the plant will be collected by the thousand and changed into drugs, it is now a protected species in many countries.

The now very rare **Butterwort** (*Pinguicula vulgaris*) grows on marshy meadows, near springs and in damp mountainous areas. Its semi-fleshy, light green leaves, in a rosette close to the ground, are shiny as if oiled on the upper side. The scientific name for the flower derives from the Latin *pinguis*, meaning fat. The leaves are not greasy, but between the elevated upper edges of the leaves is a sticky substance which attracts insects. The leaf closes over its prey and digestive juices break down the soft parts of its body. After digesting its food, the leaf once again opens.

The butterwort blooms in June and July with a single purplish-blue flower, having a double-lipped corolla running into a spur at the back. Together with another carnivorous plant, the **Bladderwort**, it belongs to the order of *Utriculariaceae*.

The carnivorous bladderwort is a hunter of tiny water life. Its name is derived from the Latin *utriculus*, meaning bladder, for its bladder is its 'fishing tackle'. The bladders are easily visible on the threadlike leaves, and look similar to roots. However, the plant lacks roots. From the confusion of green submerged stems and delicate leaves,

a long, stemlike arrangement of flowers coloured golden yellow grows sparsely from June to August. The **Bladderwort** (*Utricularia vulgaris*) and other similar species, float freely on stagnant, sun-warmed waters.

The ensnaring apparatus of the bladderwort is completely different from that of the dry land mechanism. The hollow bladder works on the principle of a suction pump. The bladder is closed by a lid with bristles so that pressure can form within. When a small animal touches the sensitive bristles, the lid is released and the bladder opens. In that moment, a stream of water pours in, carrying the prey with it and stretching out the sides of the bladder. The catching and digesting of the prey takes a short time. Within 15 minutes the bladder is ready for its next catch. It feeds in this way up to 100 times a day.

A clump of bladderwort can be up to 2 m (6 ft) long. When pulled out of the water, the 'hungry' and full bladders can be seen to be differently coloured. In one such clump about 150,000 small victims — gnat larva, grubs and tiny fish fry were found.

The bladderwort propagates mainly vegetatively, from pieces of the stem and from buds, which spend the winter on the bottom. It grows in stagnant muddy waters throughout the northern hemisphere. The whole family numbers about 200 species, which grow everywhere except in the arctic regions.

The fascinating carnivorous plants have always attracted explorers. Here are: (1) Butterwort (2) Pitcher plant (3) *Aldrovanda vesiculosa* (4) Venus flycatcher (5) Bladderwort (6) Round-leaved sundew with an enlarged part of the leaf.

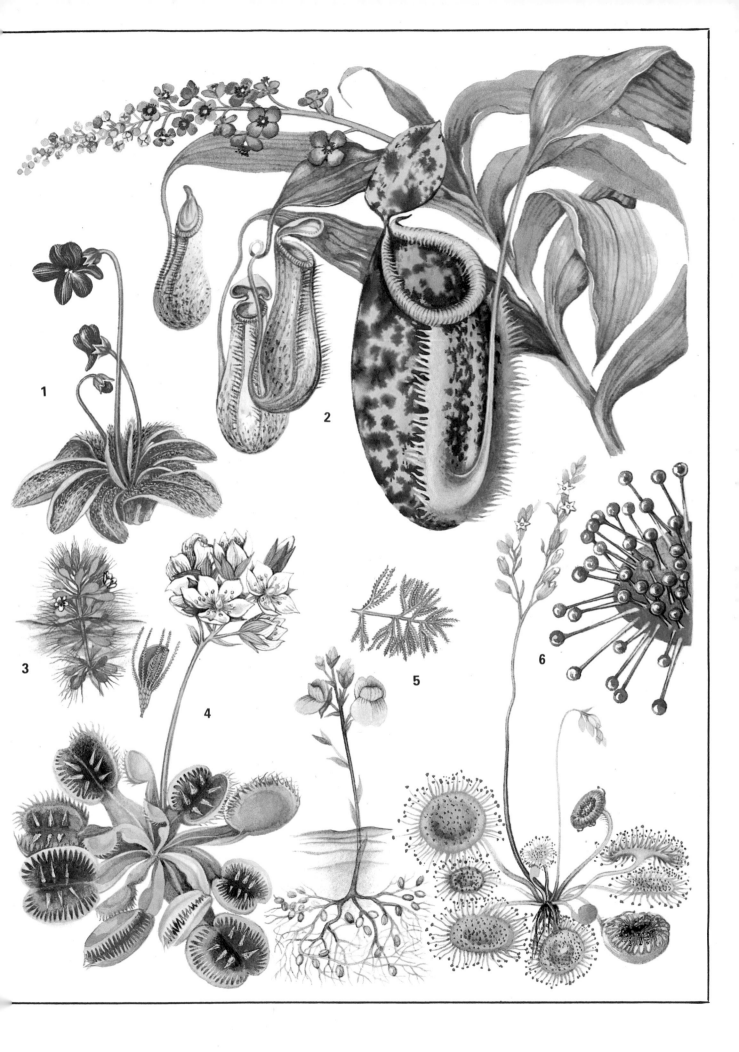

1

2

3

4

5

6

The *Aldrovanda vesiculosa* also catches its prey in still waters, though its manner of doing so is quite different. It uses the principle of a closing trap. The round edge of the leaf is folded over at the centre rib to form a sort of shell. There are sensitive, pointed teeth along the edges of the leaf blade, and bristles and glands on the inner side, secreting digestive juices. When the living creature touches the sensitive bristles, the two halves of the leaf slowly start to close. The struggling movements of the victim, as it tries to escape, stimulate the other bristles and the leaf closes completely. However, the plant does not react to non-living objects. A chance grain of sand will stimulate the leaf only partially. It will not close completely round it, for there is no point in wasting its valuable digestive juices.

The carnivorous aldrovanda is a perennial plant. Its sparsely branched stem, 10—30 cm (4—11 in) long, is constantly submerged. There are no roots, and the stems intermingle on the surface layer of the water, like those of the bladderwort. The aldrovanda occasionally blooms with a tiny flower on a thick stalk, but this is a rare phenomenon. In central Europe, the seeds almost never ripen. The plant therefore propagates through pieces of the stem and winter buds. They spend the winter in the mud at the bottom of the water and when it warms up in the spring they start to grow. When the young plant eventually exhausts the store of starch in the bud, it rises to the surface. The aldrovanda grows in the shallow and shaded waters of Europe, central Africa, India and Japan.

Nature does nothing without a purpose, so much so that some of her creations have more the appearance of a work of art.

The decorative, reddish-yellow containers (pitchers) of the **Pitch-**er plant (*Nepenthes*) are an ingenious piece of equipment. If we were to award first prize for trapping in water to the bladderwort, then on dry land the prize would go to the family of pitcher plants for its very sophisticated and also beautiful trapping equipment.

The leaves are long-stemmed and have a strong central rib passing through their flat part extending into a long tendril carrying a pitcher. On top of the pitcher is a lid which emits a fragrant and attractive nectar. The fragrance, the colour and the nectar lures insects to the pitcher leaf, as they do in many other flowers. The insects lean in to reach the nectar, slip on the smooth rim, and fall inside. Within are digestive juices in which the insect gets drowned. The plant digests what it can of the insect.

Pitcher plants are large climbing bushes. Like vines, they twist their tendrils around nearby trees, and are commonly found in tropical Asia. They grow on marshy and sandy soil, deficient in nitrogen, which they obtain from the bodies of their prey. The pitchers hang in the air on long tendrils or are situated on the ground.

The whole genus of Nepenthes has around 70 species. Their pitchers vary greatly in size — from 5 to 50 cm (2—20 in) — and in colour, being either very bright or transparently white.

Another shell-like trap is the American **Carnivorous flycatcher** (*Dionaea muscipula*). It is a perennial, 15—20 cm (6—8 in) tall plant, growing in the mossy bogs and damp lands of North Carolina. The ravenous flycatcher does not catch only flies but also other insects, complementing its poor source of nutrition.

The perfect snare is made up of the two vessel-shaped leaves which are linked by a joint. Each half has three sensitive bristles that react to the movements of the prey. When the prey moves, the two halves of the 'shell' close and the toothed edges meet each other. The leaf blade remains closed until the insect has been killed. The insect is pressed and treated with a solution similar to digestive juices.

The leaves are arranged in a rosette which is constantly growing. New leaves are endlessly being formed because each leaf takes 8—14 days to digest its prey. It can do this three or four times, after which it withers.

A Thief on a Tree

A potentially dangerous fungus grows in coniferous forests. It is the **Honey fungus** (*Armillaria mellea*). It grows in large clusters and soon fills the baskets of fungi gatherers. It is a popular fungus, recognizable by its honey brown cap, being particularly suited to pickling in vinegar, though it is not

A clump of Honey fungus.

the best of the edible fungi. However, raw or not properly cooked, it can be poisonous.

The autumn-ripening fungi are an indication of which decaying tree stumps and sometimes even living tree roots, are covered with its spawn. The fine white spawn is hidden in a broad fanshape under the bark of the trees and tree stumps and, on dark nights, make it shine mysteriously. The ribbons of the brownish-black spawn are up to several metres long and can pass through the soil to other trees and stumps. They are the storage system for nutrients and other substances which form the fungus. The spawn can grow for several years under the bark without being betrayed by surface fungus. The honey fungus grows rapidly and the wood attacked is thoroughly destroyed until it crumbles.

The **White mistletoe** (*Viscum album*) only grows on the branches of deciduous trees while another species, *Viscum laxum*, grows on conifers, pines and firs. However, plants of the order of *Loranthaceae*, including the white mistletoe and the yellow-berried mistletoe, can only grow on a certain tree or bush. White mistletoe grows on apple trees, birch trees, poplars and the like, but rarely on the oak.

The round bushes of the mistletoe settle into the crowns of trees, like birds' nests. In fact, birds are interested in these 'nests' only in December, when the white berries of the mistletoe ripen. The birds eat the seeds of the berries which pass undamaged into their droppings. Should the seed drop onto a suitable tree, it forms a small disc, which holds onto the wood by suction. There is also a wedge-shaped plug, from which grow the threatening roots, spreading into the living wood from where they draw their food.

Mistletoe can be best observed in the winter when the leaves of

the trees have fallen and only the evergreen mistletoe remains. The stiff leaves stick out from the short trunk which forks into the branches, just one new branch being added each year. The leaves of the related yellow-berried mistletoe (*Loranthus europaeus*), which grows on oaks, fall in winter.

The Australian Christmas Tree

The family of *Loranthaceae* includes both parasitic and semi-parasitic plants which are completely, or only in part dependent, on nutrients supplied by the host plant. Included in the group are related plants, such well-known European plants as white mistle-

The seed of White mistletoe **taking root on the branch of a tree. Note how the mistletoe puts out special 'stems' or haustoria, which draw nourishment out of the branch.**

Bunches of Mistletoe grow in the crowns of trees.

A flowering *(top right)* **and fruit-bearing sprig of** Mistletoe.

toe and yellow-berried mistletoe, as well as an almost unknown plant of Western Australia called ***Nuytsia floribunda.***

This is a sturdy tree growing up to 12 m (39 ft) tall with leathery and fleshy green leaves. But while it appears to be self-supporting, absorbing its own food, its hidden underground roots are sent out into the environs to feed off neighbouring grasses.

Because of the quantity of delicate, light orange flowers with long filaments and styles which ornament the tree just at Christmas time, the popular name for it is the Christmas tree. The plant got its scientific name in honour of the Dutch seafarer Pieter Nuyts who was the first to land on the west coast of Australia in 1626.

Without Roots and Greenery

The saying goes that 'Frost does not burn the stinging nettle' but it can be destroyed by a tiny plant, the **Dodder plant** (*Cuscuta europaea*).

The seedling of the young dodder plant takes hold of its future victim. As the threadlike plant stretches out, it grips the stinging nettle with tiny suctions through which it draws nutrients from the host. It then pulls away from its own root, which it no longer requires. It winds around and 'hangs on the neck' of the nettle which upholds and feeds it. Remnants of leaves can be seen on the non-green dodder plant as tiny scales. The dodder plant grows, the nettle droops, withering under the weight of the flourishing dodder plant. Eventually, it bends to the ground where the seeds of the dodder plant are scattered, bursting into life the following spring when they will attach themselves to their future providers.

There are about 30 species of the dodder plant. They come from the Old World, but some of them have already found their way to North America.

A charming parasite on the roots of deciduous trees, hazel, alder, hornbeam and beech, is **Toothwort** (*Lathraea squamaria*). It flowers in the spring, in April and May, in the rose-coloured cluster of flowers with lipped corollas. The smooth stem of the plant is also pink. The aboveground leaves are scaly and are also pink. The underground leaves are fleshy and hollow, white scales growing over the strongly branched rootstock. It weighs several kilogrammes. At the spot

The flower cluster, or inflorescence, of the **Australian** Christmas tree.

where the rootstock touches the roots of the tree there is a swelling. This penetrates under the skin of the root from where the parasite now feeds. The fruits of the toothwort are pods containing dark seeds the size of poppyseeds. They can germinate only when they come into contact with the roots of the host deciduous trees.

Broomrape does not have any trace of the green colour of chlorophyll, either. Similar to toothwort and dodder plant, it is fully adapted to a parasitic life style. The size of the parasite depends to a large degree on the amount of nutrients the host can supply. The amount of seeds produced are an indication of the determination with which broomrapes propagate. In a handful of ripe pods, a single plant produces as much as several thousand seeds. Yet they are so small they can hardly be detected by the naked eye. Clouds of seeds, as light as a feather, are carried into the surroundings by the wind,

Toothwort **flowers in spring, and can be found in the undergrowth of thickets.**

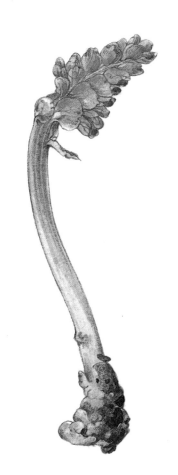

The flowering Dodder plant **twisting round a host tree.**

and the rain washes them through pores in the soil to the roots of plants. And that is the moment when only that seed which falls on its 'own' host plant has a chance to germinate. Quite often the flowering plant only appears above ground after a number of years.

There are several species of broomrape, and each lives on a certain host plant. The **Golden broomrape** (*Orobanche lutea*) attaches itself to a type of **Lucerne** (*Medicago falcata*) and to clover. It grows on sunny slopes in warm places.

131

The parasitic broomrape develops underground where the swollen part of its stem attaches itself to the root of the host plant. From the host it draws water and nutrients. In the summer a waxy stem appears above the ground, covered with tiny scales in place of the leaves. For a short period in May and June an erect cluster of yellow flowers with yellow stigma in the funnel-shaped corolla appears. Dry plants darken to a beige colour.

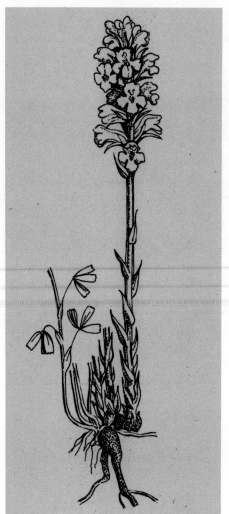

Golden broomrape **on its host plant.**

IX PLANT INTOXICATION

The knowledge that there are plants that contain poisons and narcotics is almost as old as mankind itself.
(H. L. Edlin)

In Vino Veritas

The climbing bush the **Grape vine** (*Vitis vinifera*) winds its way through the cultural history of mankind. It was one of the first cultivated plants to get into Greek legends, linked to Dionysus, the god of wine and the grape harvest. Dionysus, crowned with the grape vine, strides cheerfully through the world accompanied by a frolicking train of satyrs (men who are half

A comparison of the grapes of the wild forest vine *(left)* and cultivated grapes.

A map showing the world distribution of the main grape-growing regions.

Rÿwij Wÿnne.   Vitis Vinifera.   Weinreß.

An illustration of the grape vine in a mediaeval herbal (Matthioli, 1562).

freshing fruit are golden, golden-green, blue, purple or even reddish. Their flavour and fragrance vary according to species. The grapes are pressed for their juice.

When wine is produced, this juice is allowed to ferment rapidly in vats which creates alcohol. Later the wine is fermented again in barrels. The dried berries of the sugary grape are eaten as raisins or currants. The hard seeds of the grapes also have their use. As late as the end of the last century, the seeds were washed after the wine pressing, dried and crushed in special mills to obtain a colourless oil which gave a light that did not smoke.

The strong column of the trunk grows to a great height, the huge crown of leaves spreading like birds' feathers. The decorative leaves of the **Date palm** (*Phoenix dactylifera*) are 2—5 m (6—16 ft) long. Within the crest of the arched spread of the leaves there

A grape vine: (a) One-year growth (b) Two-year wood (c) Head of the bush (d) Root system (e) Main shoots (f) Side shoots (g) Dew roots which grow just under the surface of the soil. Fruit is born only by shoots growing from one-year wood on two-year growth.

horse and half goat). He teaches people to cultivate the grape vine and to make a drink from its heavy bunches of fruit. Another name for the god of the grape vine is Bacchus. In Athens, a day was set apart for a festival in honour of the popular god 'the Great Dionysia', with plays and a 'Rural Dionysia', including dancing and singing.

The honouring of the divine patron of wine was transferred from Greece to Thrace. Even ancient Semites and the Aryan Hindus knew the intoxicating power of wine. Wine was a sacred beverage in Egypt where they cultivated the

vine in 3 500 B.C. During the reign of King Tutankhamen, wine was drunk only at celebrations and religious rites. The wine was made from dates, pomegranates or grapes.

The grape vine prospers best on the sunny terraces of vineyards facing south towards the sun. Each year, the bushes are cut back, and the new shoots are tied to supports and pinched back to encourage more growth. Near dwellings, the grape vine is allowed to cover walls and patio roofs like a vine. The round or oval berries in the dense clusters of re-

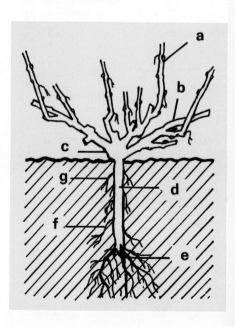

Preparing for the grape harvest.

fruits. A cut into the flower head or trunk causes a juice called 'lagmi' to run. Palm wine is made from fermenting the syrup and the juice.

Palm wine called 'taru' is produced from the boiled sugary juice of the *Phoenix silvestris* palm, which grows through the whole of India. *Phoenix canariensis* is an ornamental palm, which grows in the sub-tropical parts of the world, and also in the greenhouses of the temperate zone. However, the yellow-brown fruits of this palm are dry and inedible.

Rice (*Oryza sativa*) is one of the basic cereals of the world. In east Asia it is not only a food but a drink. A mixture of yeasts and moulds are used to ferment the rice to make saké, the Japanese national drink. It is heated and drunk warm. The light but intoxicating saké is a golden-brown liquid produced from best quality rice and water. The fermentation

is a cluster of small flowers. Later, the flowers are replaced by the fruits — single-seeded berries.

Dates are floury, fleshy and sweet, and are shaped like a plum. The very hard seed has a deep furrow running lengthwise. A date palm bears from 10—15 clusters and one cluster has up to 200 dates. In one year the tree provides from 50 to 100 kg (110—220 lb) of dates. The sweet flesh of the ripe fruits contains 60—70 per cent sugar. It is a very common fruit tree in north Africa and western Asia. It provides greenery and shade in desert oases that have underground water. The dates also supply the daily food for the native peoples. Elsewhere they are eaten as fresh or dried fruit. A syrup called 'date honey' is obtained from the pressed

A Date palm, and a close up of a bunch of dates.

takes place in the cold winter months so that the liquid will not be ruined. This is done in a special place called *saké-gura,* where a constant low temperature is maintained by the construction of thick walls and small windows.

The manufacture of saké dates back a very long time in Japan. The exact date when it started is not known but, according to ancient Japanese mythology, saké was originally the sacrificial wine of the gods.

From the 8th to the 12th centuries, manufacture was in the hands of the emperor, as was also the manufacture of paper and tea. Later, manufacture of the wine started in Buddhist monasteries and in Shintoist temples. From the 15th century the drinking of saké spread to ordinary people, and it became the national custom to drink it on ceremonial occasions.

Rice is one of the basic cereals and is the staple food for a large percentage of the world's population.

Fiery Water

Spirit is a strong, intoxicating drink, which is very popular amongst white people. This strong form of alcohol, obtained from plums and other fruit, is not very old. We find first mention made by Aristotle, but it was the mediaeval alchemists who first spread news of its attraction. The Arab physician Jabir (c. 721—815 A.D.), the father of Arabian alchemy, known also under the Latinized name of Geber, describes a distillation process and the manner in which the fumes of heated wine, which are then cooled again, become liquid. Thus, in the 13th century, there was already in existence a recipe for the preparation of *aqua vitae* from white wine. The alchemists looked upon pure alcohol obtained through distilling as a most valuable 'herbal quicksilver'.

Not only were the remarks of the alchemists appreciated by physicians and pharmacists, who prescribed the new medicine by the drop, but the preparation of it gradually turned into large-scale manufacture. The production of the first spirits was recorded at the beginning of the 14th century in France. With the expansion of technology in the 18th and 19th centuries, the production of spirits

A Japanese *saké-gura,* where rice wine is fermented.

Fruits of the Plum tree.

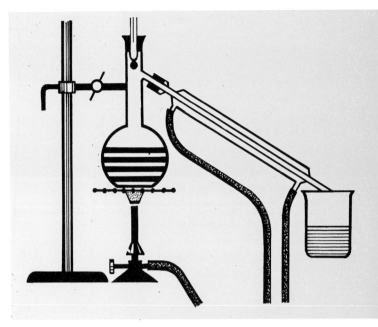

A distilling apparatus for making spirits. The liquid in the closed bowl is heated above a flame to boiling point. Gradually it turns into a vapour, which then passes into a water cooler. As its temperature drops, the vapour forms a pure liquid which now drips into a vessel. The less easily vapourized elements of the liquid remain in the first bowl.

was also expanded. A quantity of kinds and brands, many of them still existing to this day, came into being. They were the result of the distilling of various fermented fruits such as apricots, peaches, grapes, apples, palm and rice wines, cherries, rowan berries, juniper berries, raspberries, wheat and also honey and spices.

One of the well-known spirits is plum brandy, made from the distilling of fermented plums. Plums are grown in plantations and gardens and along roadsides; the food and chemical industries eagerly wait each year for the ripe fruits.

Narcotic Substances

Hemp (*Cannabis sativa*) is one of the oldest plants used by man. Although it has become best known as the source of the narcotic drug

The top of the female Hemp plant. On the *left* is an enlarged female flower, and to its *right* is the male flower.

A wooden container for opium belonging to a member of the Konjak tribe.

in the Orient where narcotics took the place of drinking alcohol, which was forbidden by the sacred writings of the Muslims in the Koran.

An unusual plant juice which is able both to heal and destroy a man is contained in the lacteal glands of a fragile plant, the **Opium poppy** (*Papaver somniferum*). When young the charming flowers, 10 cm (4 in) in diameter, have four light-coloured petals concealed within the two sepals of the calyx. The buds droop but straighten up as they open, throwing off the covering of the calyx and spreading out with a striking dark

Opium poppy **with a detail of an unripe poppy-head shedding milk.**

hashish, or marijuana, it is also a textile and oil-giving plant.

Hemp is an annual plant with inconspicuous male and female flowers separated on different plants. The 'hen' plants are much larger than the 'cockerels'. Only the female plants are grown for spinning fibres. They have a stem which is up to 4 m (13 ft) high, and broad palm-shaped leaves. The small flowers change into capsules covered with the hard, shiny, dried calyx. They are the main component of bird seed used to feed exotic birds. The dried plant is included in the official list of medical herbs of many countries.

Hemp was cultivated as a narcotic and oil-giving plant in 1000 B.C. in India and the Orient. According to Chinese records, knowledge of this oldest narcotic plant goes back to 2000 B.C. It is grown in tropical and sub-tropical regions as Indian hemp for the resin-like substance exuded by tiny glands on the leaves, the ends of the branches, and from the cluster of female flowers. The narcotic hashish has an intoxicating effect at first, but later destroys living organisms.

The use of hashish has its roots

circle at the bottom. The cask-shaped ovary, with the star-like stigma sitting on top, grows larger after fertilization to form the globular poppy-head. It contains up to several thousand tiny, kidney-shaped seeds. According to the species, they are white, pink, grey, greenish, blue or black. Only the ripe seeds contain no alkaloids which otherwise impregnate all other parts of the plant.

The white juice of the plant, termed latex, flows out when the unripe poppy-head is cut, drying and hardening in the air. It changes into a poisonous brown substance called opium. The better known of its side products are morphine and codeine. In its pure state, morphine is a drug that sends a person to sleep, eases his pains and deadens his sense of pain. It can do much to help the sick but it can also kill. The misuse of opium as a narcotic has spread from eastern Asia to Europe and America.

The ancient Sumerians (4000 B.C.), the Egyptians, Greeks and Romans, all knew and cultivated the opium poppy as a medicinal and oil-bearing plant. As expressed in its Latin species name *somniferum* — from the word *somnus* — meaning sleep, and *fero*, meaning I bring, the poppy was a plant bringing sleep and dreams. In mythology, the god of sleep, Hypnos, wears a poppy garland.

Man has grown *Barley* right from the very earliest times. Look at the map *(top right)* to see where it is grown today. Two-rowed barley is generally grown throughout the temperate zone. Less common are four-rowed, multi-rowed and other barleys.

International Beverages

A cereal plant that is immeasurably old is **Barley** (*Hordeum*). Even in antiquity its grains (which contain starchy proteins, sugars and fats) were boiled and roasted. The grains grow on a flower cluster which is about 15 cm (6 in) long and is covered with long bristly awns.

Two-row barley is generally grown throughout the temperate zone of the world. It will grow at high altitudes, in the Himalayas up to 4,000 m (13,130 ft) above sea level, and selected sorts are even cultivated beyond the Arctic Circle. Barley is ground to make flour in Tibet and is then mixed with strong tea and butter to form balls called *tsamba*. This is the staple diet of the Tibetans. In addition to two-row barley, many-row *(var. polystichum)*, six-row (*var. hexastichum*), four-row (*var. tetrastichum*), bare (*var. nudum*) and others are all grown.

Barley was known to the Asiatics at least 7,000 years ago. The oldest findings from around 2800 B.C., in Egypt, the Mediterranean and Asia, show that they not only knew barley and cultivated it, but made both light and dark beer from it. For the Egyptians and the Romans, barley was less valued as a cereal. They did not grow it as a cereal but for its malt for making into beer. It was renowned as the gift of the god Osiris. They were aware of its intoxicating properties, judging from a mention on an ancient Egyptian papyrus: 'How greatly must a man avoid beer (heg)!' But he does not seem to have done much to avoid it when written records tell us that the alocation of beer for the royal court was 130 jugs a day, and for the Egyptian queen 5 jugs.

Barley is a cereal that has always been drunk more than eaten. In Rome, barley bread was provided for the poor, the gladiators, and soldiers undergoing punishment. On the other hand, fermented barley was popular. The grains of selected, improved varieties of barley influence the quality of the beer. The grains are first allowed to germinate. The sprouts are then removed and the malt is dried. It is then crushed, mixed with warm water, boiled, cooled, beer yeast from *Saccharomyces* is added, and the liquid is left to ferment.

The fermentation process changes the sugar in the young beer into alcohol. The young beer is allowed to mature for several weeks or months, according to the strength and the quality desired. The final phase in the brewery process is the syphoning off of the beer into containers — barrels, bottles, cisterns and tins.

However, barley is linked to a much stronger alcoholic beverage — the well-known whisky. This drink of Scottish origin dating from the 15th century was, and still is, manufactured from cereals, mainly barley, and the malt made from them. In Islay the green malt is dried in peat smoke which gives a special fragrance and taste to

The female plant of climbing hops with the cone-like flower cluster. The male flower *(bottom left)* **and female** *(bottom right)* **do not grow on the same plant.**

Maté **shrub**.

The end of the summer in the hop fields.

the spirit. Good whisky is stored from 7 to 10 years to mature. It is said that the best water for diluting the spirit is water from a spring arising in red granite or one flowing through peat.

The **Hop** (*Humulus lupulus*) is the spice of beer, giving its bitter taste and helping it to keep. From the huge climbing plant, all that is used is the negligible yellow powder found in the female flower cluster. It contains a bitter, resinous substance, lupulin. Only the useful plant, the female, is grown in the hop fields. The male plant is not allowed to grow in the hop fields or in a large area around. It would ruin the female hop cones because, when they are fertilized, they disintegrate. The drug from the hop cones has been used as a medicine since antiquity. It aids digestion and stimulates appetite.

The hop is a rough, hairy, climbing plant, found growing among the coastal bushes and alder woods of Europe and Asia. But this essential raw material for beer manufacture is now cultivated in suitable places almost all over the world. With its stranglehold, the hop suffocates the bushes it climbs on, as wolves throttle sheep. That is why the ancient Romans gave it the name *lupulus salictarius* — the wolf on the willow.

The image of the wolf is still part of the species name.

Green Tea

In addition to the **Holly** (*Ilex aquifolium*), which is used as Christmas decoration, there are several

A brew of maté tea is drunk directly from the leaves on the bottom of a barrel-shaped vessel by sucking through a bombilla tube, which has a hollow ball on the end that has been punctured with holes.

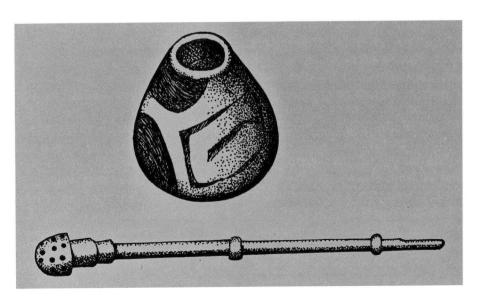

useful species of this plant in South America, especially the Maté shrub (*Ilex paraguariensis*). A tea prepared from its leaves is the daily drink of people living in South America, especially in Brazil and Argentina. The tea has a long tradition — the South American Indians used to collect the leaves of the maté shrubs which form dense undergrowth in the forests.

Before the green maté tea can be made, it is necessary to cut sprigs of the plant covered with long, oval leaves. The fresh leaves are twice passed through fire — once to wither them, and the second time, after fermentation, to dry them. The crushed green tea leaves, *yerba màtté*, have a smoky smell. The refreshing, stimulating drink is prepared by scalding the tea with boiling water. Like 'true' tea, it affects the nervous system, having a calming effect while sharpening the senses. It contains citric acid, sugar, traces of essential oil and vanilla. For the South Americans, maté tea has the same effect as Chinese or Indian tea. The latter is prepared from the dried and fermented leaves of the tea shrub (*Thea chinensis*).

Cola tree yields caffeine-containing kola nut*(below)*.

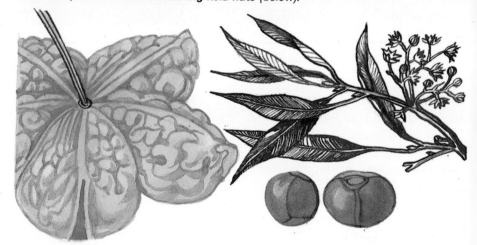

Cola acuminata.

Black Lemonade

The American soft drink coca-cola is one of few drinks drunk all over the world. But while everyone knows what they are drinking, they do not always know what it contains. The name of the dark drink with its quantity of bubbles in instantly recognizable, narrow bottles, has two parts, being the names of the extracts from two different plants.

The basis for this soft drink comes from the seeds of a west African tree, the *Cola acuminata.* This tree, and also the *Cola vera* and other species, are grown both in Africa and in Brazil. The raw material for production of the drink are the cola seeds, often called

nuts. They are held singly in the five-part wooden pod, shaped like a star. The leaves of the seeds, and especially the seed bud, contain the stimulating substances so well known in coffee, tea and cocoa. The seeds also contain tannic acid, starch, proteins and sugar. The drink made from them is stimulating and refreshing, as are the seeds when chewn.

Scientists believe that while caffeine is a stimulant for man, it has a different importance for the plant. The chemical contained in the coffee and tea bushes, as well as the coca bush, is a natural insecticide, killing harmful insects.

The Calumet

Four hundred years have passed since **Virginia tobacco** (*Nicotiana tabacum*) was first brought to Europe. It was in 1586 that Francis Drake (1540—1596), a buccaneer and later the Commander of the British Navy, returned from the New World bringing the tobacco plant to Europe. Until that time there were no smokers in the world, except for the American Indians who have smoked from time immemorial. Evidence of this has been found in the tombs of the Aztecs and in the graves of the ancestors of North American Indi-

Four hundred years have passed since Virginia tobacco was brought to Europe. Before this time there were no smokers in the world, except for the American Indians who have been smoking for as long as can be remembered. The map shows where Virginia tobacco is cultivated today. *Below:* (1) The plant (2) Its flower (3) An Egyptian water pipe (4) An Indian peace pipe.

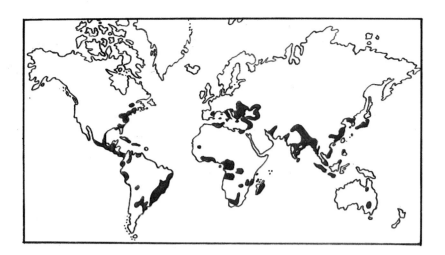

ans. A quantity of pipes of various shapes have been found which were used for smoking dried tobacco leaves as part of religious rites. The ceremonial smoking of the pipe might originally have been undertaken on agreeing peace treaties, at declarations of war, and for giving thanks to the Gods.

The Indian pipe is usually called the pipe of peace because it signalled a negotiated peace after the end of a battle. It is also known under the French word *calumet*, which refers to the pipe's similar shape to a shepherd's flute. Tobacco was considered to be a magic herb, driving out demons from the sick, and lifting the witch doctor into ecstasy so that he could govern supernatural phenomena. With the arrival of the white man, that which had once been sacred to god and exclusive to the priests, went into general use.

Virginia tobacco is a sturdy plant, growing up to 3 m (10 ft) tall, with pinkish-red funnel-shaped flowers. The parts used are the large leaves, from which are made tobacco for smoking and chewing, and snuff. However, the plant contains a number of substances which are poisonous to man. The most dangerous poison is the most important content of tobacco — nicotine. It needs only 0.05 g of this poison to kill a man. Tobacco smoke is also harmful, which is why smoking in many public places is now strictly forbidden.

Drying the tobacco leaves.

The Betel plant (an engraving from the beginning of the 17th century).

Narcotics

South-east Asia provides another intoxicant. Here the local people seek out the leaves of the **Betel** (*Piper betle*), which is a close relative of the common spice black pepper. They spread the dampened leaves with quick lime from the shells of snails. Then they wrap up in the leaf a piece of the betel nut, the fruit of the palm *Areca catechu*, sometimes perhaps a piece of bark, producing the so-called *pinang* now ready for chewing. It has a very strong flavour, which some people might not like.

In her book *The Skull Hunters*, Milada Ganguli (Prague, 1965) describes the life of members of the tribe Konjak on east Indian territory, between the valley of the River Brahmaputra and the border of neighbouring Burma: 'Dobhashi Chingom settled down near the fire and chewed betel. He always carries a supply for himself and his friends in his bag. The Konjak people love to chew the betel leaf, filled with pieces of the bitter bark of the betel palm. They cultivate the betel bushes both for their own needs and for a brisk trade in the leaves. Alongside the reed mats, betel leaves are the main product carried by this tribe to market in the marginal district of Assam, where they exchange

them for cheap tea and salt.'

There are about 650 species of the pepper plant growing in the Asian and American tropics. Most of them are climbing bushes or plants, with striking flowers. The fruit is a berry. Many kinds are cultivated including the betel. Its origin is in Indo-Malaysia.

An intoxicating pepper (*Piper methysticum*) grows on the Polynesian Islands. It is grown for its fragrant rootstock which is chewed as a drug. An intoxicating drink is prepared from the root and coconut milk, which is called *kawa-kawa*.

The 'nut', which is wrapped for chewing in the betel leaf, is the seed of the palm *Areca catechu*.

The unripe seeds contain a red dye and brown tannic acid. Together, they colour the saliva red and turn teeth black. The seeds are cut into rings, roasted, wiped with lime and wrapped into betel or tobacco leaves. By chewing the bitter-tast-

The fruit and seed of the *Areca catechu* (Betel).

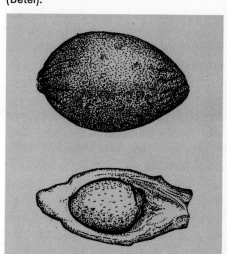

A copper container for the lime paste which is spread on betel leaf.

Areca catechu (an engraving from the beginning of the 17th century).

in the damp gorges of the mountains of Peru and Bolivia. The scientific name of the plant is derived from the Greek word *erythros*, meaning red, and *xylon*, meaning wood, founded on the flesh-red colour of the inner layers

leaves, whose shape is reminiscent of the leaves of the **Common privet** (*Ligustrum vulgare*). The flowers are tiny and inconspicuous and of no importance to man.

However, man is interested in the leaves, which is why he culti-

The true Coca with flowers and fruits.

ing lump, a chemical is released. It stimulates digestion and alleviates tiredness.

The areca palm is grown in the tropics. On its thin, 10—15 m (32—49 ft) tall trunk it carries a sparse crest of coarse leaves. They protect the small fruit, no bigger than a walnut. The seed, in its rough, fibrous covering, is sold as areca or betel nuts, but only in areas where areca and betel palm are cultivated — that is, in India, Burma, Malaysia, Thailand and Ceylon.

It is not the complete truth to say that the European does not know coca, for its species name is part of the popular soft drink, coca-cola. It is also linked to the narcotic drug cocaine.

The **Coca** (*Erythroxylon coca*) grows as a bush or a tall slim tree

of the bark. The wood itself is only tinged with red or yellow. The rodlike branches with scaly sections, typical of the coca, carry stemmed

vates coca. Coca was a sacred plant for the Incas and coca plantations were greatly revered. The leaves were chewed by ancient

A man chewing Coca leaves (a clay figure from Ecuador dating from the early 17th century). *Right:* **An ancient Peruvian pot for storing Coca leaves.**

Peruvians and their descendants still like to chew them. To prevent them from disintegrating too quickly, they mix them with quick lime and knead them into balls. Cocaine, the substance contained in the leaves, produces very pleasant feelings.

In its pure state, cocaine was for a long time very useful in medicine. It prevents feelings of pain because it paralyses the nerve ends. However, because of its poisonous side effects on the brain, it has been replaced by similar, artificially produced chemical substances.

Cocaine poisoning is serious and can kill. The fatal dosage is just 1 gr.

Banisteria caapi belongs to a large family, with 70 of its species growing in the tropics of South America. It was once believed that the plant could communicate with the dead. The South American Indians hunt the plant for use as a narcotic drug, and after taking it believe that they can see through a wall or a layer of soil, as through glass or clear water.

Boiling the plant produces a narcotic drink which the Indians call *ayahuasca*, *yaga*, *caapi* or the Amazonian 'wine that inebriates the soul'. It is one of the substances that cause hallucinations. The narcotic vine grows in the impenetrable forests of Brazil, Peru, Ecuador, Venezuela and Bolivia.

One of the four plants which gain a destructive hold over the body of those who fall victim to their narcotic poisons, is the cactus. The **Peyote cactus** (*Lophophora williamsii*) thus takes its place alongside the hashish of hemp, the morphium of poppy, and the lysergic acid in ergot.

The soft, flattened globe of the cactus is completely without thorns. Its smooth grey-green surface is ornamented with tufts of short white hairs. The 'head' of the cactus sits on a surprisingly thick, turnip-like root. The part of the cactus sought is the neck where the root becomes a thick stem. Cut up and dried in thin rings, it is a narcotic drug. In the USA they are called 'Mescal buttons', in Mexico *pelyotes* and, by the Indians, *chikuli*.

The small cactus grows in the semi-desert of north Mexico and south Texas. Most are collected in the north Mexican state of Coahuila around the village of San Jesus. It is the ritual drug of the ancient inhabitants of Mexico. They collected it with reverence as the 'intoxicating substance of the gods', and valued it as highly as a god. The drug contains seven substances, mescalin being the one responsible for the intoxicating, hallucinogenic effects. The dried mescal buttons are chewed by the local peoples, although they have an unpleasant, bitter taste. A cactus measuring only a few centimetres can cause greater intoxication than alcohol and the effect lasts from two to three days before fading. The Germans call this cactus *schnapskopf*, meaning brandy head. A person using peyote at first has pleasant sensations of joy and certainty, and loses feelings of hunger, thirst and fear. The drug evokes colour and sound hallucinations. Later come disorders of the mind and paralysis of the body.

How do they go fishing in Peru? They do not have the customary

Banisteria caapi.

How are fish caught in Peru? Not with the usual angling equipment but with a barbasek, the native word for the Lance pod plant. The sap of the plant is obtained by crushing. It is diluted with water, creating a drug which 'knocks out' the fish, or even kills them. They are then easily hauled out of the water. Fishermen use another plant, the *Derris elliptica*, with equal ease. Its root system is illustrated, *bottom right.*

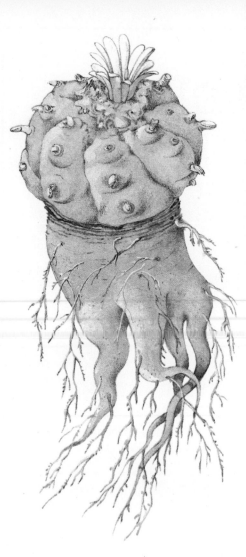

fishing line and tackle but they take a *barbasek.* That is what the local people call the herb-like plant **Lance pod** (*Lonchocarpos nicou*). It contains a narcotic substance rotenon, which is harmless for man and warm-blooded animals, but effective for fish and insects. The fishermen throw the juice, or a powder from the crushed plant, into the waters of a quiet pool where it immediately dilutes. After a while they are easily able to pull out the drugged and dead fish.

Fishing is equally simple with another vetch plant, the *Derris elliptica,* which grows in Indo-Malay-

The narcotic 'Mescal buttons'.

sia. This wood liana is 5—10 m (16—32 ft) long. Its root poison does not only kill fish but is a reliable and natural insecticide for farmers, who use it against harmful insects. It also kills parasites such as fleas, lice and tics.

The Peyote cactus **with its turnip-like root.**

X TRADITIONAL AND POPULAR FLOWERS

It is not only works of art and architecture that are a part of the culture of a nation, but flowers and trees too, showing its sense of beauty, harmony and tradition.

Sakura

Visitors to Japan are enchanted by the spring beauty of the sakura blooms, no less than by the festivities in honour of the flowering trees. The branches are lost in the shower of small blooms. The charm of the blooms of the **Japanese sakura** (*Cerasus japonica*) exceeds that of the European cherry. However, botanically it is one of the cherries and was earlier called Japanese cherry. The blooms have a larger number of petals but they do not result in fruits. The colour of the blooms ranges from pure white, through yellow, to deep pink.

The spring 'flood' of sakura blooms, spreading from island to island, from the warmer south to the colder north, lasts almost one whole month. The Japanese are so excited by this marvellous sight that they follow up reports about the advance of the blooms to make excursions into the countryside observing the sakura blooms, *no-hana*. It is a cheerful festival when the good mood, accompanied by singing and dancing, is enhanced by the drinking of rice wine saké or beer.

The national festival of excursions to see the flowering sakura is an old tradition. It is so old that it is not even known when it started. No doubt, it began in the Japanese countryside when the farmers held a ceremony under the flowering sakura, asking god for a rich harvest. The Buddhist religion makes a comparison between the brevity of human life and the fleeting beauty of the cherry blossom.

Peony

The **Chinese peony** carries the name of the country that most admires it in its Latin name, *Paeonia sinensis*. In more recent times it has been named *Paeonia albiflora* or *lactiflora*, the white peony, according to the original colour of the flowers. It is the mother plant of the so-called Chinese and Japanese peonies, popular in the gardens of Asia, Europe and America. However, the flower is most popular in the Far East, where men collected it from the mountains of northern China, Manchuria and the reaches of the Amur River.

From the natural forms which have always been grown in China and Japan, a large number of species have been developed. It was quite late, the beginning of the 19th century, before they came to adorn European gardens. The yellowish white, rose-pink and red peonies also gained favour in America where their admirers founded The American Peony Society. This society amassed a collection of over 1,000 known forms

Flowers of the Japanese Sakura.

An oriental illustration, featuring a Peony.

and Chinese artists depict its flowers with light strokes of the brush.

Chrysanthemum

The year 1989 is the 200th anniversary of the growing of chrysanthemums in Europe.

The **Chrysanthemum** (*Chrysanthemum hortorum*) is botanically one of the composite flowers, its tiny flowers forming a single flower head. The original home of the chrysanthemum is China where it has been grown as a decorative flower since 500 B.C. Nevertheless, it took second place to the peony in popularity. It was only much later that the chrysanthemum came to Japan from the mysterious, closed-off world of China. Some reports say it was

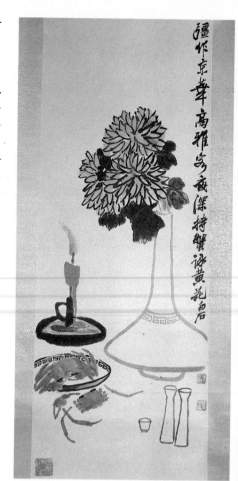

Chrysanthemums in oriental art.

Small-flowered and large decorative ▶ varieties of *Chrysanthemum*.

and shapes of the peony, and helped to improve them. The number of species today has exceeded the 1,500 mark.

Gardeners refer to two groups of species. One is derived from the Chinese peony and has large and densely full flowers, while the Japanese peony is far simpler. The yellow anthers of the stamens of the Japanese flowers are strikingly exaggerated into tongue-shaped, twisted petals.

Eastern Asia is the home of the admirable 2 m (6 ft) tall, **Bush peony** (*Paeonia suffruticosa*) and the yellow flowering peony *Paeonia lutea*. Ancient Chinese poets sang the praises of the peony, which figured in many Chinese legends, in the 8th century, but there are accurate records making it clear it was the 12th century. Japanese gardeners quite soon outstripped the Chinese experts. They expanded the 160 Chinese species to hundreds, including some very bizarre shapes.

It was only in 1789 that a French merchant from Marseilles, M. Blanchard, brought the small flowering chrysanthemum from China and so began its cultivation in Europe. However, the hearts of Europeans, especially of the French and English, were captured by a new flower which a French voyager, Robert Fortuné, brought from Japan in 1860. He brought 15 large-flower species of chrysanthemums. This was the start of an avalanche of cultivated species of the most fantastic shapes, colour and size. Up to the present day more than 10,000 species of chrysanthemum have been bred. Among them we find 'flowers' of almost all colours except blue, up to 45 cm (18 in) in diameter, and one plant with more than 1,000 flower heads on large bushes or small trees measuring 5 m (16 ft) across.

Although Europe, and the south of France in particular, became the second home of the chrysanthemum, it is still the fairytale flower of the Orient. And Japan is the country with which it is most associated. The chrysanthemum is its national flower, being a symbol of the sun and life. The name for the chrysanthemum in Japanese is *kiku*, meaning the sun. The image of the flower was used to decorate the Emperor's sword in 1186, and a 16-point symbol of the flower became the emblem of the Imperial court as well as the Japanese state emblem. The highest Japanese order is the Order of the chrysanthemum. This extraordinarily popular flower which comes in many forms has been an inspiration to scores of Japanese art-

ists and features in many songs and poems.

In the autumn, when the chrysanthemum is in bloom, exhibitions of the most beautiful flowers are held in many places in the world. In Japan, a flower festival called *kiku-no-seku* is held in honour of the chrysanthemum. And the ninth day of the ninth month is the festival of the queen of Japanese flowers.

Eastern countries admire chrysanthemums not only for their appearance but also for their taste. These flowers are a fragrant and spicy addition to many traditional dishes in Japanese, Chinese and Korean cookery.

Lotus

The carpet of green leaves of the **Lotus**, interspersed with the co-

loured beauty of the flowers, has enchanted both the Egyptians and the Indians. It is not an easy matter, nevertheless, to discover the history of the lotus flower. This is because the name lotus has been used for a number of water plants, especially the **Egyptian lotus** flower or water-lily lotus (*Nymphaea lotus*), and the **Sacred Lotus** of India or the nut-bearing lotus (*Nelumbium nuciferum*). The name lotus appears in the ancient Greek term the Lotus-eaters.

Homer wrote about the legendary land of the Lotophagi in the ninth poem of the *Odyssey*. They were the inhabitants of the northern coastal area of Libya. It proved later, though, that they were not living off the seeds of water-lilies, but the honey-sweet fruits of the **Lotus tree** (*Zizyphus lotus*) whose date-size fruits are

Large-scale cultivation of the Lotus.

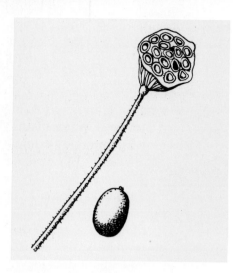

The fruits of the Lotus are nuts.

still popular in the Mediterranean region.

The Indian lotus is not just an ancient, sacred plant but a crop providing food. The rhizomes of the lotus, as thick as an arm, are starchy, sweetish, and edible. The boiled stems are used in the national dish, curry. The Indian lotus was also cultivated in Egypt. From here its fruits were exported to Greece and Italy as 'Egyptian beans'. Even the beauty of the pleasantly-scented, white to pink flowers is not just a feast for the eyes. After pollination the flower receptacle turns into a soft, spongy disc in which a number of hard nuts are contained in pits. These nuts are edible, either fresh, roasted, or ground into flour.

The marshy banks of the River Nile were the habitat of another water-lily — the Egyptian lotus flower which does not have the round, shield-shaped leaves of the Indian lotus, and which has a fragrant white flower, open from the evening until the morning. In addition to the white flower, the Egyptians had a blue lotus which bloomed during the day. Both lotuses were considered to be sacred as well as useful plants because of their edible, starchy rhizomes and edible seeds.

The Egyptian lotus flower is a native of Africa but through cultivation has established a home in Asia. The nut-bearing lotus grows in the marshy areas of the southern reaches of the River Volga, in Iran, southern Asia, Japan and north-east Australia.

Carnation

The **Pink** or **Carnation** (*Dianthus caryophyllus*), which means 'the flower of the gods' in Greek, came to Europe from the warm sunny south. In its southern Europe homeland it is a perennial. In more northerly regions it is grown as an annual or a bi-annual. Its single red flower and delicate perfume have made it one of the most popular of the fragrant flowers.

An old legend describes how the first flower with a particularly spicy fragrance was sought in the Mediterranean region by Louis IX (1214—1270) on his second crusade in 1270. He was seeking among the local vegetation a herb that would cure the epidemic plague in his military camp. The pink did not manage this task and the king himself caught the disease and died, but the crusaders brought back the flower with them, to France, in his memory. From then on, the carnation has been a favourite flower of the French, although its cultivation did not start until the 15th century. It is connected with the Renaissance, an artistic movement which spread from Italy through north and west Europe. The Renaissance brought with it an understanding and passion for the beauty of flowers. First place went to a local flower, the carnation. It became the symbol of the Renaissance, and found its way into the arts and European gardens.

The canvases of many painters show a portrait of a man or a woman holding the noble carnation in their hand. A Lucientes Goya (1746—1828) portrait shows the Marquis de Pontejos holding a carnation, like Jean-Marc Nattier's (1685—1766) depiction of Madame Louise de France holding a red carnation. The famous artist Titian (1477—1576) also painted his daughter Lavinia with a bowl of fruit on which lies a lovely red carnation. While the carnation adorns women like a jewel, on pictures of men it is a symbol of mature manhood and independence. The development of the cultivation of the carnation can also be followed on paintings.

Carnations, traditionally used for ceremonial occasions.

The traditional Tyrolean carnations *(right)* **adorning Alpine cottages** *(above)* **are increasingly being replaced by climbing geraniums.**

the white carnation of Mother's Day. In France, admiration for the carnation was at its height in the second half of the 17th century. The carnation also found its admirers and growers in England, Belgium, America, Germany and in Bohemia. To this day the famous Chabaud carnations carry the name of the Toulouse professor.

A delightful arrangement of tulips.

In a painting by Jan van Eyck (c.1395—1441) from the middle of the 15th century, a man is holding a fashionable carnation with a single flower of five petals. On the portrait of the merchant Gisz, which Holbein the younger (c. 1497—1543) painted, almost 100 years later, the blooms of the carnation are now large, full with many petals. Carnations are often found on paintings by the Dutch masters of the 17th century, on pictures of saints and as stylized ornamentation for hymn books.

Carnations became very popular in the Romance countries, especially in France where it became a national flower. It was linked in French history with the Bourbons, the French revolution of 1793, and also with Napoleon I (1769—1821). The red carnation became the symbol of the working class and

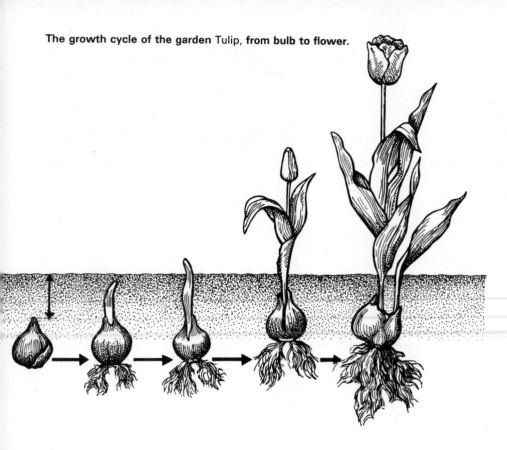

The growth cycle of the garden Tulip, from bulb to flower.

Peculiar drooping carnations, about 1 m (3 ft) long, with pinkish-red blooms, decorate the wooden buildings of the Alpine countries. The Tyrolean or Swiss carnations are a typical ornament adorning their window shutters and balconies. The damp air of the high mountain icefields keeps them fresh.

Tulip

The **Tulip** (*Tulipa gesneriana*) was the sensation of the second half of the 16th century. It was not only a rarity for the growers but also for merchants. It became an object of speculation. The events surrounding the first tulips in Europe can be compared with the gold rush in the American west. The prices of tulip bulbs rocketed with a single

A flower market in the Netherlands.

bulb of a rare species priced at one to several thousand Dutch guilders. Yes, Holland really did become the country of the tulip. Even so, it was in Holland that the tulip appeared in Europe for the first time. The place where tulips were first grown in Europe was Prague, at that time the residential city of the Emperor Ferdinand I (1503—1564).

The first tulip bulbs were brought in 1554 to the Austrian Emperor by his ambassador to Turkey, A. G. Busbecque, as a gift from the Sultan of Turkey. From there the tulip spread to other European countries, and also to the Dutch who are still enchanted with them. From Prague they found their way to Vienna, Italy, France and, in 1582, to England. Carol Clusius, a Viennese professor, left in 1573 for the Leyden University in Holland. He took tulip bulbs with him and so their cultivation began particularly around Haarlem, where they grew well. They soon became highly fashionable, with tulip-growing even turning into a craze. At its height, a single bulb of a new species was priced at 13,000 guilders. It was nearly a century before the 'tulip crash' came and the price dropped to reasonable limits.

The tulip comes from the Orient, Turkey and Persia. Originally, the Turkish sultans held tulip festivals in their gardens. Older Persian forms of tulip brought to Europe were accurately described by the Swiss botanist Conrad Gesner (1516—1565). It was in his honour that Linné named this whole group of large blooming tulips *Tulipa gesneriana*. Many of these so-called botanical tulips, which were not very successful at first, are now among the gems of flower gardens. They have their habitat in central and western Asia, and around the Mediterranean. Their blooms open on quite short stems very early in spring.

Narcissus

A flower of the ancient legends of the Greeks and Romans, the *Narcissus*, was a funereal flower for the Greeks. On the other hand, the Chinese held it as a symbol of

A 'flood' of golden Daffodils is one of the finest sights of spring.

155

The growth cycle of the garden Daffodil.

kept by the English Daffodil Society in 1910 contains 2,150 cultivated species of the narcissus. Their colours ranged from white, strong lemon yellow, to orange. Another delightful flower is the daffodil, with a creamy white perianth and a salmon pink corona.

The narcissus remained in Great Britain. Together with the leek, it became the national emblem of Wales. Scotland has the thistle, Ireland the shamrock and England the red rose.

Sugar bush

The bushes of the 60 species of the genus **Protea** (Sugar bush) have their home in the South African Cape province. The narrow, leathery evergreen leaves grow thickly along the branch that ends in a splendid cluster of flowers. The small-lipped flowers are densely grouped in the flower head, similar to that of the clover or composite flowers. Instead of bracts, it is supported by large, red-coloured leaves. The fruits are

purity and joy in their New Year celebrations. The narcissus is a flowering bulb from the family of *Amaryllidaceae*. Its home is the area around the Mediterranean, where it grows on mountain meadows and on damp slopes.

In the middle of the 16th century when Europe began to know and adore tulips, only two kinds of narcissus were grown in European gardens — the white and yellow. In 1614, the narcissus was still a great rarity in the garden of the pharmacist K. Porret, in Leyden, Holland. And when C. Clusius discovered the *Narcissus tazetta* near Gibraltar, and another species, the *Narcissus jonquil*, near Seville, the modest bulb set out on its road to glory. The number of narcissus species increased with the improvement and cross breeding of the natural species. They prospered best in Holland where there are particularly favourable conditions for the cultivation of bulb flowers. The Dutch traded mainly in the *Narcissus tazetta*, which they used because they could force it into early growth.

The narcissus found its way to England shortly before Queen Elizabeth (1533—1603) came to the throne in 1558. They became so highly fashionable that they turned into a collectors' craze. A record

The remarkable beauty of the Sugar bush.

hairy nuts containing one or two edible seeds. Flowers of some of the species contain scaly nectaries which attract insects.

The nectar-bearing flowers, white or reddish in colour, grow on the bush or little tree of the **Sugar bush** (*Protea mellifera*). It dates back to the tertiary period when the order was at the peak of its development, and many related families also grew in the northern hemisphere, in Europe.

These lovely woody plants now only grow in the southern hemisphere, mainly in South Africa, Australia and New Caledonia. Sugar bush and many other of this genus grow in the remote mountains near the Cape of Good Hope in South Africa. These flowers have such an unusual appearance that they have become the national flower, and are used to decorate glassware, dishes, and so on.

Many sugar bushes are grown in glass houses in the northern hemisphere as sub-tropical and tropical plants. They do well provided they are given the conditions of their homeland — a damp winter with low temperatures and a dry summer.

Index

Page numbers in italics refer to illustrations